DON WILTON
FOREWORD BY GREG WILTON

SEE YOU AT THE
FINISH LINE

NELSON BOOKS
A Division of Thomas Nelson Publishers
Since 1798

www.thomasnelson.com

Published in Nashville, Tennessee, by Thomas Nelson, Inc.
www.thomasnelson.com

Nelson Books titles may be purchased in bulk for educational, business, fund-
raising, or sales promotional use. For information, please e-mail
SpecialMarkets@ThomasNelson.com.

See You at the Finish Line!

ISBN: 0–8499–0353–X

Printed in the United States of America
1 2 3 4 5 6 — 09 08 07 06

This book is dedicated to Rob, Greg, and Shelley Ann.
The race is set before you;
I'll see you at the finish line.

ACKNOWLEDGMENTS

No effort of this kind can possibly be undertaken without the extraordinary assistance of extraordinary people.

I thank my wife for her sustaining love and encouragement throughout my journey thus far toward the finish line. I thank my sons, Rob and Greg, for being true men of God. I thank my daughter, Shelley Ann, for her steadfast spirit. I thank my daughter-in-law, Annabeth, for loving my son. I thank Sam Davis for his persistent guidance and organizational leadership as my friend and partner in the ministry. I thank the Knights of the Round Table—Steve Skinner, Steve Wise, Lee Foster, Clint Smith, Britt Dillard, Kent Holt, John Young, Sam Davis, Eddie Robertson, Sal Barone, Scott Stancil, and Seth Buckley—for their covenant of true love and friendship in our life journey as we strive toward the finish line together. I thank Jimmie Davis for her initial and significant effort to harness the intent and purpose of this book. I thank Cristie Wisecarver for her extraordinary dedication and undeniable giftedness in seeing this task come to fruition. I thank Sharon Brisken for her constant willingness and continual availability. I thank the members of my wonderful church, the First Baptist Church of Spartanburg, South Carolina, for the privilege of serving with them as we all set our sights on finishing well. I thank the board of directors of The Encouraging Word broadcast ministry for pouring themselves into this ministry which seeks to help all who listen to find the Savior, without whom it would be impossible to see one another at the finish line. Above all I thank my Savior, the Lord Jesus Christ, for His grace toward me as I willingly endeavor to submit to His divine will so that I, too, may see all of you when we all cross the finish line. And so shall we forever be with the Lord Jesus!

FOREWORD

Greg Wilton

My father is a man of a thousand adventures—adventures which elevate my curiosity about what it truly means to live a full life. I've always wondered how one man could accomplish so much in one lifetime.

When I think about my dad, stories immediately begin to flood my mind, making me feel as if I were reading an epic novel about some famous historical figure. I remember him telling stories about his days as a young boy at boarding school in South Africa. I imagined my dad was the sort of kid whose thirst for adventure could never be satisfied. Surfing the wild coast of Africa with his brothers, riding bikes in Zululand, camping for weeks in isolated parts of Africa without any luxuries. These were the adventures my dad encountered while still a child.

My dad's adventures intensified as his independence increased. From working on pig farms to enlisting in the South African army, my dad never let a day go by without accomplishing something worth remembering.

He still practices this mentality today.

Eventually his adventures would lead my mom and him to move to America because God was calling him to an even greater adventure. This would become the focal point of his life as my dad soon discovered that the greatest adventure in life is to pursue God fervently wherever He leads.

God led my dad to New Orleans; faithfully, he followed.

My dad, together with my mom, showed up there with nothing except the dream of searching for the fulfilled life—a life such as people can find only when they search for God with all their hearts. Years of walking by faith has made my dad who he is today, and I can truly say that I have no greater hero and role model in this world than my own father.

As I was beginning to live out my own adventures with increased independence, at first I doubted the authenticity of my dad's stories. I never thought my dad was a liar; I just thought it was impossible to fit so many adventures into one lifetime. It would honestly take me several lifetimes to accomplish what my dad has accomplished with his. Surely no one could do so much with so little time. Is living life to the fullest really possible?

But then I began to think about my dad's character.

As far back as I can remember, my dad has always said this phrase to my brother, sister, and me: "Have I ever let you down?"

My answer to this question directly correlates to the authenticity of my dad's past adventures. No, he has never let me down because not to live his life to the fullest would mean that he never gave his best to God. My father has always surrendered and submitted everything to God. Therefore, a life of mediocrity has not, is not, and will never be an option.

Now I believe with all my heart that my dad really is the man of a thousand adventures. He's never needed to prove this to me because his actions are always the litmus test. Today, God's glory is my motivation to live the fullest life possible, and my dad is the living illustration.

This book speaks about living life as an adventure unto God. Within these pages you'll discover how one can truly live a full life from start to finish. Every moment in life, every inhale and exhale, every thought and every action, when given to God in complete submission to His will, is truly the greatest adventure known to man. My father, whom I affectionately call Big Chief, is living such a life, and there is no one more befitting than him to share such wisdom.

Thanks for never letting me down, Big Chief.

PREFACE

This book is a series of ramblings about the race of life. Think about this for a minute. Life is tough! I know this from personal experience. At the best of times, life is tough. From the day we are born into this world, we come under instruction. It's tough enough being alive. It's tough enough being a child. It's tough enough being an adolescent. It's tough enough being a teenager. It's tough enough falling in love. It's tough enough getting married and having children. It's tough enough making a living. It's tough enough burying our loved ones. It's tough enough being alone. It's tough enough being a Christian in a lost and dying world. It's tough enough knowing what to do and how to act but not being able to do and act. It's tough enough going to church on Sunday but having to live in the real world on Monday. Yep! We are constantly under instruction. Most of it is good. Especially from our mothers and fathers and those who love us. But much of the advice we are given is not so good. And so with the good and the bad all mixed up we still have a race to run. Life goes on. It won't stop. Not for anything. The clock is ticking, and with every passing second we find ourselves just one second closer to the finish line.

Being a Christian makes all the difference because the Holy Spirit empowers us and the Word of God teaches us how to finish well. My paltry ramblings will only make sense when rooted in the foundation of God's Word. This is the lamp which lights our pathway. This is the means by which we can run the race of life, fight the good fight of faith, and finish well. Read on road runners! I'll see you at the finish line!

CONTENTS

THE FIRST CHAPTER

Ready to Run: An Introduction

"For I know the plans I have for you," declares the LORD,
"plans to prosper you and not to harm you; plans to give you hope and a future.
Then you will call upon me and come and pray to me, and I will listen to you. You
will seek me and find me when you seek me with all your heart."

—Jeremiah 29:11–13

It was a bright and sunny Tuesday morning. Nothing much to speak of was happening; nothing out of the ordinary was going on. It was just another unremarkable day. People were getting up, getting ready, having their morning coffee, reading the newspaper, and heading off to work. This unassuming Tuesday morning was unfolding like any other typical day, or so it seemed. The date was September 11, 2001. It all started about 8:30 a.m. Four airplanes were hijacked. Two of those planes struck the World Trade Center buildings, one plane hit the Pentagon, and one plane crashed into a field. There were four planes; three of them hit their targets. One of them was diverted.

Etched in my memory forever will be the mental image of the two planes exploding into the World Trade Center. To this very day, my mind cannot conceive of the devastation; my heart cannot digest the evil that took place on that terribly tragic morning. I will never forget the looks of desperation on the faces of the firefighters, police officers, and emergency workers as they tried to rescue those who lay helpless in the arms of tragedy. I vividly remember watching in horror as thousands of New Yorkers literally ran for their lives. The thriving, pulsating, living streets of the city were clouded with smoke, ash, and debris. For a moment, time stood still. I can recall the words, the screams, and the gasps as the World Trade Center gave way and crumbled to the ground. My heart stopped as the television screen blackened into an eerie silence. The clouds of dust and smoke swallowed up the professional news crews and the amateur videographers. This is a day I shall never forget.

As I reflect upon September 11, 2001, I can only imagine the thoughts that must have gone through the passengers' minds in those final moments. I can only imagine the great sense of helplessness each of them must have felt. I cannot fathom what those men, women, and children must have gone through. I do not want to think about the deep pain they must have known in their hearts, the utter desperation they must have felt in their souls. I ache for those individuals. My heart bleeds for their families.

Of the four planes and the occurrences therein, we have been given the most information about the passengers and the experiences on board United Flight 93. This was the flight bound for San Francisco which tragically ended up in Pennsylvania. All accounts point to the fact that the passengers on board this flight were made aware of the unfolding events in New York City. From what we know, we can surmise that a group of people aboard this flight came to a point of some understanding that the events in New York were linked with what was happening aboard their flight. At some point, they realized their lives were in jeopardy and the plane they were on was in serious trouble. Quite possibly, some of the men and women knew that Flight 93, their flight, was the fourth in the chain of terror and destruction. I'm sure they began to speculate about their future; I'm sure they were desperate with fear over what might happen next.

We know that just before they reached Pennsylvania, several of the passengers on board had a conversation together. We do not know exactly how they communicated; we do not know exactly what they said. But we do know this— a conversation went on between certain passengers and a plan was devised. Much speculation has centered around the last-minute activities of the ill-fated passengers. Some of the speculation includes a report that some prayed first, some called their loved ones a final time, and some rustled up much-needed courage. Whatever they did in those moments prior, the time came when they stood up, joined together, and headed for the cockpit. They turned their plan into action. During this fateful flight, after the conversation had ceased, one gentleman by the name of Todd Beamer stood up and said something like this, "Guys, we know the situation. We've talked about it. Now let's roll!"

There came a specific point in time on Flight 93 when incredibly courageous people recognized it was time for action. They had *some* understanding of the situation, enough to know they might be a part of an evil, diluted plan, bigger than this flight alone. They talked with each other; they set their sights on the cockpit. They seemed to know that if the plane wasn't to end up like those in New York City, it was up to them to act. And that's what they did. Who knows what might have happened had they not taken action—maybe the White House, maybe the Capitol building, who knows what the terrorists' target was. Nonetheless, these brave, strong individuals seized the moment and did all they could to stop the attacks. They rolled!

Life is tough! At the best of times it's tough. From the day we are born, we are under instruction. Most of it is good, especially that from our mothers and others who love us. But much of it is bad. And so with the bad and the good all mixed up we have a race to run. The journey does not go away. It is always there. It's relentless. This is why we choose God's Word. This is the lamp and the light of our life's pathway. It is all good. It has no error.

This is why we will place most of our focus on Hebrews. It is clearly divided into two sections. The first is doctrinal. The second is instructional and applicable. The first section lays the foundation much like our mothers who taught us from the day we were born. They taught us truths upon which to base our later judgments. When we grew into adulthood, it was hoped we would put these fundamental truths into action. Our ability to run the race of life is, in many regards, in direct proportion not only to the instruction we received in our early days but also to our willingness to apply those truths in the daily fabric of our lives as we run the race of life. The Epistle to the Hebrews gives us a wonderful understanding of the nature and character of God in its initial proposition. The first twelve chapters of this marvelous letter set the stage for us; these verses give us the game plan. On a rather personal level, a close and intimate study of this nature truly challenges me. It is as though I can hear the Lord questioning me by making a statement and then following it up with a soul-searching question that would sound something like this: "Don, I am delighted that you are serious about preaching My Word to your people. In fact, I am pleased that you are serious about teaching the deep truths of My Word. But what I want to know is what are you doing with the Word you preach and teach?" At first, I am speechless. Then I turn to chapter 13, where I discover my marching orders. A suggested paraphrase of this practical section of the letter could read as follows: "You know My Word. I have made it abundantly clear. We've talked about it. Now, let's roll."

In the first twelve chapters of Hebrews, God tells us all about the superiority of Jesus Christ. By means of the Holy Spirit, God's Word endows us with an understanding that only comes from Him. Oftentimes when I'm studying Scriptures, I try my best to understand these truths, but it's just not there. My heart, my mind, my emotion, and my logic have not been able to fully grasp what God is revealing to me. Days and sometimes weeks later, God, by His Spirit, opens the eyes of my understanding. Through His Spirit, He gives me insight into the deep truths and mysteries of *who* He is and *what* He wants me to do. The process of gaining that wisdom from God absolutely blesses my heart every time it happens. Those "aha" moments are truly priceless because we finally *get* what God was trying to tell us all along—we have had a successful communication with our Maker! The more I know about who God is and why Jesus Christ died on the cross for me, the more my life becomes enriched, challenged, and directed. At that point, God knows I have enough understanding to be held responsible for action. I'm ready to get in the game. It is somewhat reminiscent of the time when a firstborn son, who has spent weeks dreaming about the day he will be able to drive and many more months studying the driving manual which is required for the driving test, wants to take the car out a-l-o-n-e. The father, skeptical but knowing this day must come, looks at his son, hands over the keys to the car, and says, "It's your turn now. You take the wheel." Perhaps this is what is taking place at this juncture. In the letter to the Hebrews, I believe we hear God, in much the same way as the father, saying: "I have instructed you in My ways. You have practiced and studied for this. Now, it's time to do what you know to be true. Let's roll!"

Most of us can identify with this when we think about all that's involved in the running of a race. Preparation and training are not only necessary but critical for success. As an athlete you begin by getting your training schedule, and then you devise a plan. You decide what foods you'll eat and what foods you'll skip. You read up on the subject; you talk to others who have run in similar races; you buy a new pair of shoes. And then you train. You start by running three miles. Then you increase to eight. You work in a little cross-training and stretching because you know that "prevention is better than cure." Your daily training is extended, the runs become longer, and you actually feel pretty good about this whole thing. Finally, the big day arrives—race day! It's time to put all that training, all that knowledge, those new shoes, and that last protein shake to work. In the same way, the first twelve chapters of Hebrews provide us with the background information we need in order to live a life pleasing to God. It's sort of our training schedule.

Chapter 13 presents us with those final words of advice—the pep talk we need right before a big race. Within these verses a question is implied: "What are you going to do with what you've learned so far?"

Many years ago, I was privileged to be a professor of preaching and evangelism at the New Orleans Baptist Theological Seminary in Louisiana. One of my responsibilities was to "teach preaching" to up-and-coming preachers. The classes were always rich in atmosphere and filled with anticipation and expectation. The students had converged on New Orleans from all around the country. Every one of them was as different from one another as chalk is from cheese. Some were married, and some were single. Some had multiple undergraduate degrees, and some had the basics. Some came from wonderful, strong and vibrant Christian homes and backgrounds while others arrived on campus fresh from the billiard room and the beer joint. Some had read the Bible from cover to cover while others were still wondering why Jesus had healed a bunch of "leopards," of which only one returned to say thanks! Most of them were poverty-stricken, but all of them had one common denominator. God had been pleased to call them into full-time ministry, and they had responded. I loved them with a passion, and I still do. God's choice servants, indeed.

So here they were. Gathered together on the campus of a place that had trained "preacher-boys" for generations. A place that not even the devastation of a major hurricane can deter. A hallowed place built on providence and prayer.

Just think about it. These guys were taking a class on how to preach. Do you hear how ludicrous that sounds—one man trying to teach another how to preach? Obviously, we know that it is the Holy Spirit of God working through an open and humble vessel that makes a good preacher. However, there are some basic principles young pastors can learn and incorporate into their repertoire to become more effective communicators of God's Word. Things like eye contact, proper articulation, what to do, what not to do, when not to put your hands in your pockets, when to button up your jacket, when to add inflection in your voice, what color tie to wear (not really, I was just seeing if you were paying attention; though some pastors I've seen could use a little help in that area, but I digress). In Preaching 101, we enumerated all those things related to good stage presence.

So here I was, teaching preaching at the New Orleans Seminary to a bunch of unlikely students in a classroom fully equipped with a pulpit and a congregation of self-styled experts, all of whom were only there by the grace of God. I would position myself on the back row armed with my Bible and an elaborate sheet of paper that highlighted many of the most relevant and pertinent "dos and don'ts" of the art of preaching. The student who was preaching would stand behind the classroom pulpit, ready to preach the assigned passage of Scripture. He was allotted twenty-five minutes for his sermon, and each of the listening students evaluated his preaching. At the end of his sermon, I would get up, come to the front of the classroom and publicly humiliate, uh, I mean evaluate him. All the students present were encouraged to offer words of wisdom, advice, correction, and even friendly rebuke.

One student came through my class who I really believe was probably the most gifted young preacher I had ever heard. This young man could preach with the eloquence of a tried-and-tested professional. He was right out of college, only about twenty-two years old, but when he came in there and stood up to preach, it seemed as though he had been preaching all his life. His sermon was powerful and riveting, and I told him so. My accolades were accompanied by a chorus of "amens," "uh-huhs," "come-on brothers," and "tell it like it is," all of which left the distinct impression we were in an African-American revival service. The message was one thing, but the manner in which he delivered the message was entirely another. It was effective, strong, gripping, and a blessing to say the least!

Two days later, there was a knock on my office door at the seminary. This same young preacher stepped into my office with a somewhat forlorn look on his face. He said, "Dr. Wilton, I need to talk to you." I said, "Okay, what is it about?" like I didn't know. "Well, sir, I, I don't seem to understand something. The other day in Preaching 101, you gave me the impression that I, I, I did pretty well. So did the entire class and, and you were very complimentary and, Dr. Wilton, respectfully, I'm not asking for an "A" or "B" or anything like that, but . . ." I interrupted impatiently, "Well, what seems to be the problem?" I pretended not to know because I wanted to make him work for this. "Well, here's my paper and you gave me an "F." You failed me!" I agreed and said, "Yes, that's right, brother. So what's the problem?" With his confidence fading fast, he questioned, "I don't seem to understand. The way you talked, I thought I had done pretty well, maybe even an "A" for the course, but when I got my grade, you failed me. Dr. Wilton, this is a semester-long course!" "That's right. You failed the most important part of this course; you've got to take my class all over again. It many even mean you might not graduate this coming May." The color drained from his face. "I don't understand."

I began to explain, "Let me help you. A few days ago, I was outside Blockbuster on Elysian Fields Avenue, which turns left onto Gentilly Boulevard close to the seminary. It just so happened that I was in my car at the traffic light right there at that intersection, waiting to make a left-hand turn. Directly in front of me was a seminary student in a car also waiting to make a left-hand turn. In front of him there was a car with an elderly lady sitting in it. When the light turned green, the elderly lady's reflexes were slow, and she could not get going. That seminary student honked his horn loud enough for everyone around him to hear. To make matters worse, that same seminary student rolled his window down, stuck his head out of the window, and let her have it. He did not curse, but he certainly let her know exactly what he thought about her inabilities. To make matters worse, this same person used his car as a tool to show her just how angry he was. He shot around the right side of her and then barreled back into the left-hand lane. She was still half out in the middle of the road and he looked back, shaking his fist, continuing to yell at her. A few days later, that same seminary student came to my class, stood up, and preached to us about the love of God. My friend, you are exactly correct. You flunked the course, and it has nothing to do with your preaching ability."

In the same way, each of us must answer difficult questions as we make our way through this life. Questions like, "When push comes to shove, how do I fare?", "When I run the race, am I running with perseverance?", and "When I'm sifted, how do I react?" (see Luke 22:31–32). As Christians, we must put into practice all we have learned along the way. When times get hard, when trials come our way, or when tragedy strikes, we should take hold of the things we know to be true. We must live up to what we have already attained as believers.

Paul has some poignant and remarkable insights on this. In 1 Corinthians 13:11 he states, *"When I was a child, I talked like a child, I thought like a child, I reasoned like a child. When I became a man, I put childish ways behind me."* As we grow, we must leave behind those ways, which are unbecoming to God. We are called to mature; we are called to grow. On Flight 93, the passengers had to grab hold of what they knew to be true. They had to make a decision and stand firm—there was no looking back. Philippians 3:12–16 reasons the same way:

> *Not that I have already obtained all this, or have already been made perfect, but I press on to take hold of that for which Christ Jesus took hold of me. Brothers, I do not consider myself yet to have taken hold of it. But one thing I do: Forgetting what is behind and straining toward what is ahead, I press on toward the goal to win the prize for which God has called me heavenward in Christ Jesus. All of us who are mature should take such a view of things. And if on some point you think differently, that too God will make clear to you. Only let us live up to what we have already attained.*

We must make every effort to run the race of life according to those things we have learned in training. When race day arrives, all those little decisions we have made along the way—what to eat, what not to eat, what shoes to buy, how to work through the cramp, when to let up, and when to push through—have collectively combined in attempts to ready us for the big day. But even with all the training, all the head knowledge, the best running shoes in the world, it all comes down to that day, to how we perform right then and there. You see, friends, a race is a struggle. It takes effort to cross the finish line. I know this to be true. The great men of the Scriptures knew this to be true. The Christian life is often a struggle, an effort, but one that is certainly worth the trouble. Proper training, therefore, becomes crucial in making it to the finish line. Unfortunately, life does not present us with a timetable of events. "Okay, Johnny, on November 20, 2007, you will experience a great tragedy in your life. You should begin preparing now so you will be equipped to deal readily with that situation." Boy, wouldn't that be nice! We would know exactly when the race was to begin; we could have our game faces on. But life doesn't work that way. So we must be ready *all* the time. We must take hold of what we know to be true, we must stay attuned to God's prompting, and we must seek the face of God in all we do. Then, and only then, will we ever truly know the plans He has for us. You see, God has a plan to prosper us and not to harm us, plans to give us hope and a future. But the only way we will ever find this is to continue reading in Jeremiah. Remember verse 13, *"You will seek me and find me when you seek me with all of your heart."* We've got to know God. We've got to be ready for the race. Whether we're in work boots, high heels, house slippers, or the best pair of running shoes money can buy, the race in inevitable. How will you do?

The first twelve chapters of Hebrews provide the training. They prepare us for race day. Hebrews chapter 13 gives us the much-needed pep talk. God is at the beginning with us, encouraging us and reminding us of the truths we know to be absolute. He is in our corner, cheering us on, saying, "Remember what I have taught you; it's time to roll. I'll see you at the finish line."

THE SECOND CHAPTER

The Litmus Test

"As I grow older, I pay less attention to what men say. I just watch what they do."

—*Andrew Carnegie*

"Practice what you preach," "Actions speak louder than words," "Let your walk match your talk," and "Don't speak it, live it." Sound familiar? We frequently throw these adages around in our day-to-day living. I believe there is a plain and poignant reason these idioms have maintained their popularity throughout the years: People like to see actions that are consistent with words. It's really that simple. It just makes life easier when we know we can trust the words of another person. It is reassuring to see that a person's walk follows their talk. I bet you don't have to think too hard to recall a time when someone has told you one thing and then turned right around and done something different. It's confusing, isn't it? It can be downright frustrating. When inconsistencies in the behaviors of others arise, they cause us to question their character and to second guess their integrity. We think, "If he's not following through on this, can I really trust him?" I believe most of us desire consistency in both word and deed from others. Our minds have a difficult time accepting the idea that a person would claim, "I think it is wrong to tell a lie," yet say to their boss, "I can't come in today because I'm sick," knowing all the while that the free round of golf awaiting them was the true motivation for the call. Although it is difficult to digest, sometimes it only takes one small inconsistency to cast doubt on

12

our entire character. You see, friends, our actions, *those things we do*, must be consistent with our words, *those things we say*. We all know this; we have all experienced this. I'm sure we have even been caught on both sides of this. And so I ask you: in life, do your actions pass the litmus test?

According to *Merriam-Webster's Collegiate Dictionary*, the phrase *litmus test* is defined as "a test in which a single factor (as an attitude, event or fact) is decisive." It is a test that relies on a single indicator. Whoa! That sounds like a pretty tough test. It's basically a one-shot deal. If you miss the question, you fail the exam. The litmus test is often utilized by hospitals to determine if a mother is in true labor. Special paper, called litmus paper, is introduced during an exam. If the mother's water has broken and amniotic fluid is present, the paper will react by changing colors. This is a test to determine *real* labor from *false* labor.

In life, we often face up to our own versions of this sort of litmus test. Trials, struggles, and hardships that come our way give us the opportunity to pass or fail. "But, pastor," you say, "how can I be expected to perform well on every test that comes my way? My character shouldn't be judged solely on one mishap. We all make mistakes!" I agree. I know that every last one of us will fail to react properly when put to the test. Thinking of life in terms of "pass" or "fail" is incredibly intimidating. Those are standards no one can meet. I certainly can't. "So what then, pastor? If a minister can't pass the litmus test, what chance do I have? I'm just a regular Joe. I mess up all the time." Friends, I'm not here to tell you that God is calling us to be perfect—we can't be and He knows that. What I *am* telling you is this: God has called us to strive, to roll, and to run. Paul did not say he was running a race of perfection, quite the contrary. He said rather, "I press on; I forget what is behind me and I strive toward what is ahead of me." Some tests we will pass with flying colors but, sadly, we will encounter others that we fail. So what do we do when life presents us with a litmus test that we fail?

We get real; we become vulnerable. Needless to say, I am here to tell you that I mess up too. I mess up daily. Just ask my wife, Karyn. I'm sure she has some stories to tell on me. But the fact that we mess up isn't the point. We are all guilty as charged. We will all fail at some time or another. The significance, the bread and butter of the issue is found in how we recover; it's how we get up and continue to run. It's not that we finished first, second, or twenty-fifth; it's that we finished the race. If we never own up to our inconsistencies, if we never take responsibility for our actions, and if we never correct our behaviors by learning from our mistakes, then we are all like the man James speaks about who looks at himself in the mirror but forgets what he looks like just moments later. I want to be clear on something. God has *not* called us to be perfect, but He *has* called us to strive to be perfect. Although we know we will fail, we can't let that stop us from trying. We cannot take advantage of the grace God has given us. It is paramount that we struggle to make our actions match our words. Others are watching us, even unbeknownst to us. We are examples to someone. Don't take it lightly.

When our actions overshadow our words, we lose credibility. Although our entire character might not have been shattered by one unfortunate incident, most assuredly our sincerity is called into question. It's like that tiny string on your favorite sweater. You're in a hurry to run out the door and notice a string hanging from your sleeve. You give it a little yank and . . . uh oh, it begins to unravel. The loose string has turned into a tear. Next thing you know, you're back upstairs changing clothes because that tiny nick has turned into a huge hole. Although the extreme may not always be the case, each time others witness inconsistencies between our actions and our words, their confidence in us begins to erode. The tear grows bigger and bigger. They think, "If he's not truthful about that, then what else is he hiding?" Now, don't get me wrong. Each of us is guilty of inconsistencies here and there—boy, I am! However, at some point, we have to stop and ask ourselves some hard questions: "Is what I'm saying matching what I'm doing?", "Are my actions screaming so loudly that my words have become silenced?"

The paradox between our talk and walk is one of the most difficult aspects of the Christian life. It is my single greatest struggle because I stand in the pulpit Sunday after Sunday and preach what the Bible says. I'm ready to tell people what they ought not do and yet I go home and wrestle with that very same issue. I say, "Do not eat with your mouth open," and then I'll go to a restaurant and eat with my mouth wide open for all to see. I am tested daily. Sometimes I pass and sometimes I fail. When I'm out on the golf course with my buddies and I shank the ball deep into the woods, did I pass or fail that test? Did my words match the sermon I preached just days earlier? Wherever we are, whatever we are doing, we must consider what our actions say about our character. Oftentimes, our actions are the most vocal and eloquent spokesmen of our true convictions.

If basketball games could talk, I believe many of us would hang our heads in shame. Growing up in Africa meant my children had a dad who knew absolutely zero about this incredible game. I will readily confess I had never played a game of basketball in my life. Even now, the funniest thing in the world, evidently, is to watch my brothers, Rod and Murray, and yours truly playing in a family game at Thanksgiving. But enough of that humiliation. How my two sons, Rob and Greg, became such outstanding players I'll never know! But their countless numbers of games over countless numbers of years bore witness to their dad perched on many a stadium seat. Without losing sight of the extraordinary skills of an exciting game, many a game was accompanied by the most atrocious behavior, especially from the parents who are there to support their sons and daughters. I have seen grown, church-going men who lose their witness all because a referee made a bad call. You see, our actions must match our words. Whether it's a bad call by the ref, a ball in the rough, a car pulling out in front of us, or a child talking back, we are to remain consistent. These particular points in time are examples of when we are tested. The congruence of our behaviors with our words is necessary for others to see that we are believers in Christ. These are our chances to pass or fail the litmus test.

This demand to act accordingly can cause great consternation in many a person and may produce an expected response: "But, Pastor, I know I will fail more times than I succeed. I can't be expected to maintain that kind of standard all the time. I'm just not good enough." Yep, it certainly is tough, but this is where the grace of God becomes so very special in our lives. Herein lies one of the reasons we have been given the grace of God. Let's take a closer look at the meaning of God's grace.

I truly believe God's grace has been given for two basic and essential reasons. First, in order that we might be saved from our sin and born again to newness of life. It was God's grace that sent our Savior to the cross because our Heavenly Father had mercy on us in that while we were still sinners, Christ Jesus died for us. And, second, God's grace sustains us through the journey of life. This is very important. It is the reason we find so many beautiful benedictions in the Scriptures. Benedictions are simply man calling for and praying God's accompanying grace upon the one for whom they pray. When God's grace comes on the believer, that person is covered in God's "living" mercy. This is the grace necessary for all the situations and circumstances of life that keep popping up during the race of life. If we are to see one another at the finish line, having accomplished our very best for the Lord Jesus, then we must understand the significance of our dependency on God's sustaining grace. God's "saving" grace, on the other hand, is necessary in order to receive forgiveness of sin and eternal life. Isn't this great?

God knows we lack the ability to be perfect, and being devoid of inconsistencies is what perfection calls for. Therefore, God bestows on us His unconditional, unyielding grace. Perhaps we always ought to remind ourselves that the only difference between the "best of us" and the "worst of us" is the grace of God. You see, friends, it's not about the "perfectness" with which I live this life, but rather what God teaches me about His grace during those times of struggle. God, who dwells in me, compels me to live according to that which I know to be true based upon the Word of God. Studying His Word, listening to His will, and knowing His nature will guide my actions and direct my words no matter what test comes my way.

First Peter 2:15 reads, *"For such is the will of God that by doing right you may silence the ignorance of foolish men"* (NASB). It is paramount to not only think right and know right, but to *do* right. If all you do is *know* what is right, you are no better off than the Pharisees of the New Testament. God rejects that kind of pharisaical legalism. God requires that we know the good we ought to do and, get this, actually *do* it. A church or religious denomination that teaches the wonderful deep truths of God's Word but never goes out into the highways and byways and endeavors to lead people to Jesus Christ is destined to suffer a slow but certain death. Titus 2:7–8, states, *"In everything set them an example by doing what is good. In your teaching show integrity, seriousness and soundness of speech that cannot be condemned, so that those who oppose you may be ashamed because they have nothing bad to say about us."* Your practice has supported your preaching. Your walk has validated your talk.

The need to get busy and live for the Lord Jesus Christ is vital to our Christian walk. But before we can go out and live confidently for Him, we must consider a few things. First, let's examine the basis for our actions. Let's look at the role doctrine plays in our lives. This word "doctrine," can sound a bit intimidating. All it really refers to is a group or a system of beliefs. So, I ask you—what is your doctrine? What are the beliefs you live by?

One of the great joys of my preaching ministry continues to be the privilege of preaching through entire books of the Bible. It took me sixty-six weeks to complete an incredible expository series through the letter to the Hebrews. Can you believe that? Why would I spend that much time teaching in one book? It reminds me of the age-old questions some of our high school students pose because they can't understand why they have to go to school day after day and learn about things like literature and algebra. They longingly ask, "Why do I need to study literature? William Shakespeare died in 1652; let's just leave him alone. Why do I need to read all those "thees and thous"? I don't care that Romeo and Juliet had a tragic love story; I don't care that King Richard lost his horse and he'll never get it back. Why do I need to study, 'My horse, my horse, my kingdom for a horse?' Who cares?" We all remember those days, do we not?

Why do we, as parents, push our children to study literature and algebraic equations? Why do we encourage them to find a good college to attend? For crying out loud, why make mom and dad write out all those checks for their children to get a degree? Why do we insist that they keep learning and learning and learning? Well, these are the things that equip us for life. These are the building blocks, the foundation for the future. Why did I spend sixty-six weeks preaching systematically through the book of Hebrews? Why so much time and effort? Why is it crucial to know our own personal doctrine? Allow me to provide a number of suggestions regarding the importance of doctrine:

1. Doctrine is the standard of conduct.

What you know can certainly determine how you live. It is a true statement that a weak theology will result in a weak lifestyle. If what we believe has a weak foundation, then the way we act will have a weak foundation. If a man believes God has nothing much to say apart from a slap on the wrist for adultery, then he has succeeded in justifying adulterous behavior in his own eyes. Hence the growing problem we are witnessing in so many religious groups and organizations over significant moral issues. Biblical issues of godliness and behavior soon are relegated to the opinions of man. And that is a dangerous place to be because we all have opinions. Our personal doctrine, in essence, is our code of conduct. We have this code to refer back to when life gets confusing. I like to think of the term "doctrine" as more like a personal guidebook, a map. If I am frustrated, scared, or faced with a situation for which I don't have the answers, I can look back to my code, my map, for direction. You see, friends, our doctrine, our belief system, is part of who we are. If we have a weak theology, we will have a weak lifestyle. Theology means "the study of God." Broken down, literally, "theo" means God and "ology" refers to the study of something. If you don't know God, if you don't study the Word of God, and if you don't understand the significance of doing so, then you will be a weak person; you will develop a weak character. Every wind that comes your way will blow you down. Just when you think one tornado has come and gone, another one will come and destroy your home. Do you know why? Because your foundation is weak. You have nothing solid to stand on.

Our doctrine is the standard of our conduct. It will govern the way we behave. I'm reminded of the parable about the man who built his house on the sand. When the waters began to rage and the wind began to blow, the house was swept away. In life, when the winds kick up and rage against us, we will be swept away. However, the man who was wise and built his house on the rock was able to stand firm. He had taken the time to build his house on a solid, steady, firm foundation. He was protected from the adverse effects of the angry sea. Certainly, this is not to say that he didn't experience the storm. He did. But his house didn't fall down when the waters rose up against him. The steady, strong foundation kept his home safe from the storm. Though we might sway, though our foundation might shake, if our doctrine is strong and grounded in the Word of God, we will not fall. A strong doctrine will protect us and guide us. It is the rock that will save us from the storm. Think of a huge oak tree. It is solid; it is deeply rooted. Its leaves and limbs will sway back and forth with the wind, but because of its sturdy roots and the fact it is grounded in the earth below, it will not break.

2. Doctrine is the foundation of moral judgment.

We have all dealt with a moral dilemma at one point or another. Often-times, we are forced to make decisions that bring morality into ques-tion. We ask ourselves over and over, "Is this right?" and "Am I doing the right thing here?" In the first twelve chapters of Hebrews, we exam-ine the doctrine which God has laid out to guide us. The precepts God teaches us through these chapters and across the pages of His Word pro-vide the foundation upon which we stand. We should not make our moral decisions based on what *we* think. If our decisions are under-girded by emotion, whim, or desire, then we will surely make bad moral judgments. The only true way to know if the decision we are making is right is to measure it against the Word of God. My dear friends, if I was your pastor today and I tried to lead your church based upon what *I* think, we would be in serious trouble. You and I will never make the "right" decisions *all* the time. The only way we can possibly hope to do what is right is by knowing what God's Word says. Psalm 119:9–16 re-iterates this:

> *How can a young man keep his way pure? By living according to your word. I seek you with all my heart; do not let me stray from your commands. I have hidden your word in my heart that I might not sin against you. Praise be to you, O LORD; teach me your decrees. With my lips I recount all the laws that come from your mouth. I rejoice in following your statutes as one rejoices in great riches. I meditate on your precepts and consider your ways. I delight in your decrees; I will not neglect your word.*

The psalmist, David, knew this to be true. If we do not have a strong foundation, our attempts to live according to God's way will be in vain. We will try and try but never meet the mark. Sound doctrine is the foundation of moral judgment. Hang on to that.

3. Doctrine is the passion of love.

I am so grateful to the Lord for my church. I do not say that for any form of self-aggrandizement. The people in my church are really some of the most wonderful folks you would ever want to meet! They are so gracious in giving, not only of their money but also of their time. Many of our members are involved in building churches in places like Brazil. We are busy sending people to foreign lands to serve as missionaries. We have a wonderful Helping Ministries Center that provides food, clothing, and other necessities of life for those who cannot help themselves. Our young people are actively serving the Lord in missions in the mountains of Kentucky. We have a team that travels to prisons across our country, singing about the amazing grace of God to those who are behind bars, both literally and figuratively. I could go on and on talking about the wonderful ministries of our church and the gracious people who make God's work their own life's work. But I want to take you down another path; I want to highlight a different matter. I want us to look at the motivation behind all these great and selfless acts. Let's answer the question, "Why do we do these things?"

To answer simply, we do these things because we love. That's it—it is the power of love that drives us to meet the needs of others. You see, friends, love is a strange and wonderful thing. It is an exceedingly strong emotion that powers us and propels us to do things we never imagined we could. Love can empower us to accomplish great and mighty deeds. Love can literally change someone's life. We all have the ability within us to love others and to reach out to those around us. We can all make a difference.

Love is an action word. A verb. It carries with it the idea that something is happening. It's not a tangible concept; it's not a place you can visit. In most cases, it's hard to define love; it's hard to articulate the vast meanings it connotes. Despite the mysteries surrounding this word, there are several concrete principles that we know to be true about this elusive term. We know that love is a process. We know that love is a decision. We know that in order to love, we must be selfless. We know that love can soften people. We know that love can change others. We know that to love someone else means letting a little of ourselves go.

So if I say, "Doctrine is the passion of love," what exactly does that mean? Well, it means our belief system is the overflow or the action of love. Passion is the action of love based on what we believe to be true. Therefore, it is imperative for our doctrine to be congruent with God's Word. This is the only way our love will withstand the test. Unfortunately, as wonderfully deep and abiding as our love is, it will fail to measure up sometimes. The reality is that we have limitations, even conditions, on our love. But, thankfully, God does not. We have the ability to love deeply because God loves us and He dwells in us. God is love, my dear friends. His unwavering, unchanging love for me compels me to love others. He gives me the passion to love. If I have never experienced His love, I will have no desire to do the same for others. My love will run out because it, in and of itself, is not enough. I'd be one of those people who spread a little dab here and a little dab there, but my actions will never amount to anything because I'm not compelled by the love of God to do what I do. I would merely be going through the motions.

Why do I need to study? Why is it imperative for us, as God's people, to study the Word of God? Why is it essential for young people to be disciplined in the Word of God? Why is it so important? You've got it! It is the standard of conduct; it is the foundation of moral judgment. Knowing God's Word and studying His doctrine fills me with a zealous passion to love others.

4. Doctrine is the power of godliness.

In 1 Timothy 3:5, we are warned that the time will come when people will have a form of godliness but deny its power. Let me share something important with you. In order for us *not* to pay lip service to a form of godliness, we must have the power of God upon us. Let me say it another way. In order to be a man who is driven by the power of God through the Spirit of God, I must have access to God Himself. The power of God comes through His Word and dwells in the heart of man. It is this power which drives me to live a life which will be well pleasing to Him. Without it, I will only give myself over to a form of godliness.

What does a form of godliness look like? Let's take a typical Sunday morning for example. A man comes to church and looks "godly" enough. He has his Bible in hand, he participates in worship, he speaks to his friends, and he even attends Sunday school. From all appearances, he's a devout Christian. But it really is all in the appearance. When he walks out the door, he goes back to the way he was. There was no connection made; there was no real change that took place. He simply came to church, sang a few songs, ate a doughnut, and headed out to lunch. That is a form of godliness, but it denies the power therein. In that scenario, God is denied the opportunity to break down the walls, remove barriers, and really work in his life. The man has become affectiveless; he is without emotion. He has denied God the opportunity to reside truly in him. This man hasn't understood what the power of God's doctrine can do in his life. The illusion of godliness, whether it's forged or merely an innocent habit, does not signify the inner workings of Christ in a man's life. In order for us to digest God's doctrine, and I mean really chew it up and swallow it, we must recognize the power it carries. We must realize that godliness will be an outpouring of our hearts, not a learned Sunday morning ritual. Internalizing God's doctrine will allow us to know the true power of godliness.

5. Doctrine is the indispensable mandate of Scripture.

God's Word tells us that the time will come when people will no longer listen to sound doctrine. We see it happening in America today. Many people make decisions based on what suits them best at that particular point in time regardless of how it affects others. They say, "I want it like this, and I'm going to have it like this regardless of what *you* think." It is evident that our foundation in America is gradually eroding. That is why the country no longer knows what to do, particularly in matters of morality. Some say this is wrong, other parties say this is right. Who in the world knows anymore? It is a zoo out there, my friends. A lot of talk and a lot of walk, but unfortunately the walk and the talk are incongruent.

We are living in a day and age when, increasingly in many quarters, the due diligence of education is not deemed all that necessary anymore. There seems to be a growing consensus that some individuals should be encouraged to sign on the dotted line without any concern for long-term or societal consequences. This "get it all and get it now" attitude has been compounded by the desire (and understandable need) for money. Consider the massive fortunes to be made in the world of professional sport. Up until 2006, the NBA was able to draft high school students, seventeen and eighteen years of age, to play in a man's game. Many of these kids were enticed to give up their college eligibility without the chance to experience it. They were catapulted into a lifestyle that espoused, "You can have all of this right now. No college education needed. No maturity is necessary." These young people landed multi-million dollar contracts at the expense of a college experience which this author believes is so valuable in the teaching of many of the hard lessons of life. Now, don't misunderstand me here. I recognize the once-in-a-lifetime chance these boys were given. Absolutely, I do. What I don't like is that they are no more prepared for their future than a rabbit is to drive a car. They have not even lived outside their parents' homes for the past seventeen years, and now suddenly they own million-dollar homes, have loads of cash, tons of women, and the freedom to do whatever they want to. How do you think many of these kids turn out? The same way I would—flat broke and utterly confused.

God tells us that studying and knowing His Word are indispensable mandates in the race of life. You cannot do it without it. It takes a huge amount of hard work, but that is what He requires. There are no "skipping steps" or "taking short-cuts" when it comes to studying God's Word. The idea to "get it all and get it now" does not fly with God. It is an arduous process at times to learn, understand, and appreciate the vastness of His doctrine. But if you love the Lord, the journey of learning will feel less like a task and more like an honor. Knowing God's doctrine and hiding it in our hearts is an indispensable tool which will guide us along the way.

6. Doctrine is the equipment of action.

Everything we read, study, and take notes about regarding God's Word will equip us further for life. For example: I go out and purchase a new lawnmower. I sit down and read the manual from cover to cover. I know how to crank the engine, how to lower the blade, and how to add gas when it runs out. In theory, I am an expert at cutting the grass. But when does a lawnmower really become a lawnmower? When it sits there and waits for me in the garage? Nope. It becomes a lawnmower when it performs the action a lawnmower should—when it *mows* the *lawn*. It is one thing to read about cutting the grass, but it is another thing altogether to do it.

Doctrine equips us for action. It prepares us for the big test. You see, in life we don't know if the teacher is going to come into the classroom and say, "Students, it's your lucky day. The exam will be open book." We think, "Alright! I've got the answers right here in front of me. All I have to do is find them in time and I'm all set." There are times, however, when the teacher enters the room and says something like, "Okay class, put up everything except a number two pencil. It's test time." We think, "Man, I hope I remember everything. I studied really hard, but what was that equation again?" And there are even times when we walk in the classroom, put our books down, and the teacher abruptly says, "Put up everything. It's time for a pop quiz." We think, "Oh, no. Oh, no. Oh, no."

Life is much like that literature class or that dreaded algebra class. We might be informed that a test is coming, have plenty of time to prepare, and even get to use our books. Or we might be put in a situation where we are forced to recall those equations or metaphors without the assistance of books or notes. And then, more often than not, there are those awful times when we are caught off guard—we are suddenly required to put into practice what we know to be true. Therefore, we must always be ready. This requires that we have both a "head knowledge" of God's doctrine as well as a "heart knowledge" of His Word. Ensuring that we have both our hearts and heads engaged in the learning process will lead to a passing grade when the litmus test comes our way. You see, if our heads fail us—if we can't remember that bit of Scripture, that sermon analogy, or that insightful thing our Sunday school teacher said—then our hearts will still be able to serve us well because we have not just memorized the material, but we also have digested God's Word. If we have listened intently to the Sunday school lesson, grasped those verses the pastor preached on, and metabolized what God was trying to tell us during our prayer time, then our hearts will show us the way. We have made a connection; we have had a successful communication with God; we have been equipped for action.

7. Doctrine is the candle of our light. (Yes, you read that right.)

One of my favorite sayings of the Lord Jesus was when He said: "Let your light shine before men that they may see your good deeds and praise your Father in heaven" (Matthew 5:16). We oftentimes place the focus of this directive on the action of the light shining and rightfully so. But have you ever thought about the candle? You see, the light won't shine and the flame won't glow without the wick and the wax. These two essential components of a candle provide not only the stimulus but also a place for the illumination to occur. And so it must be in terms of ourselves. We will never shine for Jesus until we have a candle to shine from. It really makes sense when you think about it long enough. I believe it's pretty difficult to light a candle if there is no candle to light! We will never be the influence in this world we need to be unless we have a strong doctrinal foundation on which to stand. Jesus Christ is our candle; His Word is our wick. He gives us the opportunity to shine, but we must first be grounded in Him.

Doctrine is the foundation. It is vitally important. But just as Todd Beamer came to the point of realization that time was no longer a luxury, we must come to that same conclusion. We need to act now. We do not know how much more time we have on this earth, do we? We must make the most of every minute we live on this earth.

It will always be one of the things I will be most grateful for when I think of Brittany Fogg. Just eighteen years of age, Brittany was tragically killed in a single-car crash not too far from North Greenville University in South Carolina. Few of us will ever forget her funeral. It was one of the most victorious funerals I have ever officiated. Don't get me wrong. Our grief was at an all-time high because we all loved her so much. Her parents are a tribute to the Lord Jesus Christ and so is her boyfriend, Lee. But looking back on her life, I think everyone will agree that Brittany ran for the finish line cherishing every day. Her every moment of life seemed to be an opportunity for action. Because of this, she has left a mark on all who came into contact with her. Her legacy will always be, "Whatever you do, run the race of life well. Make the most of every opportunity to live for the Lord Jesus Christ. And, I'll see you at the finish line!"

In Hebrews 13, God is basically saying, "Enough talk. It's time to take action!"

In the subsequent chapters, we will discover some of the actions God has outlined for us to take which, I believe, are so vital in the race of life. A good suggestion may be for you to have an open Bible before you as we study His Word together. The Bible is an indispensable and imperative tool designed to equip us in the truth of God. Everything we believe about life and everything we will come to know about God is found in the pages of the Bible. Keep it near you; keep it open. Let the Word of God speak to you as we make this journey together.

Let me add another thought. Although I sit and write the words you are reading, I did not choose the subjects covered in this book. Hebrews 13 dictated the subject matter. Perhaps this is one of the benefits of preaching and teaching through the Word of God. When you do so, you are seldom required to select the subject. The Bible does the selecting. The Bible chooses the topic. It follows that no one can ever "accuse" a preacher of "picking" on them! And, I will have you know, sometimes we come across subject matter in the Bible that, to be perfectly honest with you, we would prefer to sidestep. I would like to simply "jump over" some of these issues because they are difficult to talk about and make us feel uncomfortable. And so it is in this case. There are a few difficult topics which we will address. But I've found over the years that the best way to remove a Band-Aid is to rip it off all at once. Sometimes it is far more productive to face these hard issues head-on and see what God has to say. Ladies and gentlemen, fasten your seatbelts, lace up your running shoes, and sharpen your number two pencils. Here we go! And I'll see you at the finish line!

THE THIRD CHAPTER

To Love Like Jesus

Greater love has no one than this, that he lay down his life for his friends.

John 15:13

Scripture Reference: Hebrews 13:1
Keep on loving each other as brothers.

Throughout history, mankind has grappled with the notion of love. We have made many attempts to define such an intangible word. We have implemented tangible tools like poems, movies, art, gifts, and musical lyrics to articulate this idea of love. Even the dictionary has a definition for love. Great literature, beautiful jewelry, and sweet-sounding music try to capture the essence, the vastness of the words, but unfortunately all fall short. Love is many things, and it is defined in many ways. Some see love as giving gifts. Others view love as affection. And still others think of love as the show of selfless acts. The lyrics we hear, the words we read, and the definitions we quote can't encapsulate an appropriate description of love. In order to really know what love is, in order to understand the power love carries, I believe we must experience it. We must *feel* love in order to know what it truly means.

With this, I'm reminded of that unforgettable time when my wife gave birth to our firstborn son. It was a grand occasion to say the least. Robert Edwin John Wilton made the announcement of his intended arrival early in the morning. Karyn and I had practiced hard for this time together, attended classes together, prayed together, and keenly anticipated this momentous miracle. I cannot truly recall the journey from our home, down Interstate 10, past the Louisiana Superdome, off the ramp (at mach speed) at Clairborne, the left turn on Napoleon, and up the ramp at Baptist Hospital. I do remember wheeling my wife through the elevators and up to the sixth floor. I even remember the pain this expectant daddy felt when Karyn went through nearly seventeen hours of hard labor. I recall how clever I was to actually ask her how she was feeling, and I vividly conjure up the image of her face when I brought a dripping wet towel to "dab" her flushed face when she requested it. She told me I should have made the whole exercise a lot simpler by just filling up a bucket of water and pouring it over her head, her entire body, and then all around the room, just to make her feel better! The actual delivery of all my children was something I will never forget.

There he was! None of us can truly explain the emotions, the sense of awe, the power, and the sheer presence of a living God.

But, although I absolutely fell head over heels for our son, I couldn't hold a candle to what my wife felt. It was as if I was standing there with them in the delivery room but was somehow on the outside looking in. I was missing out on something; the puzzle didn't quite fit. As I stood in there watching her gaze at him, stroke his head, and nuzzle his body, I knew she was experiencing a love that I was yet to know. It's as if she were suddenly given a greater capacity to love right there in front of my very eyes. Watching my wife cradle her newborn son gave me the impression that she got a glimpse of something new, something like she had never known before. Over the course of several weeks, I developed that same deep connection with my son; I began to gaze at him with complete adoration. But because my wife had carried him in her womb for nine months, labored for, and delivered him into this world, she was able to experience this and appreciate it sooner than I could. I had to connect with him; I had to work at it. Karyn, on the other hand, caught a glimpse of what it is to love without limits during our son's very first moments of life. The same has held true not only for Rob but also for our other children, Gregory Donald Wilton and Shelley Ann Wilton. My love for them has not only deepened, but it has also broadened. It's like I have carried them in the womb of my heart.

Our society has tried to define, tried to articulate love. But despite its greatest attempts, the definitions, the movies, the gifts, and the displays of affection all fall short. Do you remember when *Love Story,* starring Ryan O'Neal and Ali McGraw, hit the screen in 1970? Talk about love! It was a gallant effort to articulate and define love . . . at least for a time.

The Bible, however, is the only place we can truly find an adequate and accurate depiction of love. The Bible contains God's definition of love; it demonstrates love in action. Thinking of my wife gazing into the eyes of our firstborn son is the closest, most tangible example of God's love manifesting itself in my life. I believe that an extraordinary love exists between a mother and a child. This is not to dismiss or diminish the love shared between man and wife—certainly, a strong and abiding love exists there. Furthermore, this is not to say that if you do not have children you can't experience love. Some of the greatest and most tender demonstrations of love I have ever seen exist between couples who do not have children. God translates and interprets our love. He makes the application always in the context of our individual circumstances. This is merely to point out the parallel between God's love for us and our love for our children. It is a selfless and oftentimes thankless role we play as parents. The altruistic nature of mothers is truly remarkable. It is a relationship where one person gives and the other person receives. It is much akin to the relationship with our heavenly Father. Just think about it for a minute. We ask, we plead, we beg, we take, we want, we need . . . the list goes on and on and on. It is only the very mature Christian who can stop and say, "Wait a second. *I* need to be the one to listen. *I* need to show that I trust Him. *I* need to obey the first time He prods. *I* need to give back instead of taking all the time."

Friends, the love a mother has for her child is incredible. It is probably one of the most self-sacrificing roles a person can play. And, yet, this beautiful picture of love is overshadowed by the love our heavenly Father has for us. He loves us without restraint and without limitation. *"For God so loved the world that He gave His **only** begotten Son, that whoever believes in Him should not perish but have everlasting life"* (John 3:16 NKJV, emphasis mine). God expects nothing in return except that we love Him and we love others. When asked what the greatest commandment was in the Law, Jesus replied, *"'Love the Lord your God with all your heart and with all your soul and with all your mind.' This is the first and greatest commandment. And the second is like it: 'Love your neighbor as yourself'"* (Matthew 22:37–39). Simply put: God wants us to love.

Love must be expressed both vertically and horizontally. Vertical love is a receiving love because it is that love which flows from the heart of a heavenly Father who is love. When we love vertically, we look up toward the Source of all love. That is why we place our faith and trust in Him. In so doing, we go toward God. We stand in His presence. We look to Him as the "alpha," the beginning One, the Source. And, yet, our looking to God comes in response to His looking for us. He, alone, is the initiator. By His Spirit, and through His grace alone, we are drawn toward Him. And when we are with Him, we receive from Him!

The horizontal expression of love comes because God has blessed us with many opportunities to develop earthly relationships so we can experience a portion, a sampling of love. But in order to truly know love, we must know God. It really is the matter of the cart and the horse. Respectfully, God is the horse in that our relationship with Him determines the content and quality of our relationship and capacity to love our fellow man. We simply won't have the capacity to love others if we have never experienced the love of God first. Man and wife, sister and brother, mother and child, or a closely knit friendship can give us a taste of love on earth, but until we know God and experience the love He has in store for us, our earthly relationships will miss the mark. We will never be able to love like Jesus until we have accepted His love for us.

Perhaps this is the essence of 1 John 3:14–15, where we are told that our relationship with God is in direct proportion to our relationship with our fellow man. *"We know that we have passed from death to life, because we love our brothers. Anyone who does not love remains in death. Anyone who hates his brother is a murderer, and you know that no murderer has eternal life in him."* (I refer you to my book, *Totally Secure*, which gives a more thorough explanation of this directive.)

Let's consider this a little more in depth. I believe it will help us to contextualize what is about to be outlined in this chapter. A closer look at verse 14 mandates a closer look at the very meaning of our salvation in Christ Jesus. The fact is we can know we have "passed from death to life" based on the fact that we love like Jesus. Passing from death to life is exactly what happens when we look up to God and receive His love into our hearts. Remember that God is love. This is who He is. And, so, when God gave us His only Son, He did so as an act of love. The giving of Jesus was the ultimate expression of His love in terms of action, but in so doing God was also giving Himself because He is love. It follows that if Jesus is God, and He is, then the One who gave Jesus is the same One who gave Himself. When we receive the Lord Jesus into our hearts and lives as Savior and Lord, we receive and become that which God is. Love! John makes the connection by pointing out the means by which we can know we are being saved is based squarely on the fact that receiving Christ is receiving God, who is love. In question form, how is it possible for men or women to say they have a personal relationship with God and yet not demonstrate His love to others?

Now, a point of clarity is necessary here. The word "brother" is neither gender exclusive nor is it selectively inclusive. The early Christians commonly referred to themselves as "brothers" and "sisters" in Christ.

The term was used by those who were of "the family of God" and made direct reference to the fellowship of people born into the same spiritual family under the headship of God the Father. Now God the Father has expressed His love toward all who believe in Him. Jesus was sent to this earth to die for all who would come into a right relationship with Him. God loves His own. He loves His children. In a sense, He cannot help but love because He is love. This is His character. And, so it is with all who profess Christ as Savior and Lord. We love like Jesus because the love of Christ dwells in us. His life is our life. We are in Him, and He is in us. If, in fact, we do not love our fellow believers, we are fakes. We are not who we say we are. We "remain" in death. And this reference to "death" is the same reference we find in Revelation 20:14: *"Then death and Hades were thrown into the lake of fire. The lake of fire is the second death."* If the first death is a physical death, then the second death is a spiritual death. Should Jesus not come before our time on earth draws to a close, then we will all suffer physical death. In fact, we are born to die, and our physical death is a direct consequence of sin. In Paul's first letter to the church at Corinth (1 Corinthians 15:22), we are reminded *"in Adam all die."* Here both physical and spiritual deaths are brought together in that all sinners who have rejected the saving grace of God are condemned to die in their bodies physically and in their souls spiritually.

Let's also remember that it is impossible for a born-again Christian to suffer death for a second time. The second death spoken of in Revelation 20 is exclusively soul death. Conversely, the mandate given by our Savior to Nicodemus in John 3 to be "born again" is the hallmark of God's saving grace. Being born of the Spirit ushers in the making of God's new creation through the sacrifice of His Son, the Lord Jesus Christ. Hence, Paul could follow up his statement concerning man's Adamic nature with *"so in Christ all will be made alive"* (1 Corinthians 15:22). The preceding verse helps to explain this more clearly. *"For since death came through a man, the resurrection of the dead comes also through a man."*

And so our relationship with God is the fundamental issue here. We love like the Lord Jesus because He first loved us. Love is the character of God, and we, who are His children, must therefore carry His genes, so to speak. It's kind of "like father, like son!"

Hebrews 13 is a trail filled with directives. In the very first verse, we find the command to love our fellow Christians. This is the initial thing God tells us to do as we run the race of life. I think that is the key—it is so simple and yet so remarkable! God's Word is literally exhorting us to love! As we have established thus far, believers in Christ have experienced His love and are capable of loving others. So, as believers, we are ready to put love into practice. We are ready to love like Jesus. I would like you to consider three reasons God puts such emphasis on loving fellow Christians:

1. Love is the evidence of our faith.

If you are a Christian, you are a member of the body of Christ; you hold to the Christian faith. This means that love should be the standard-bearer or the identifying banner of your life. Love is the evidence of our faith; it says that we ascribe to God's Word and God's way. If we call ourselves Christians, the world will know this to be true because of the way we love others. In John 13:34–35, we read, *"A new command I give you: Love one another. As I have loved you, so you must love one another. By this all men will know that you are my disciples."*

For many years now, I have traveled to various places across the United States with one of my closest friends in the ministry, Steve Skinner. We have served the Lord together, not only in New Orleans, but also in Spartanburg, South Carolina, for many years. Steve directs both Yesterday's Teens and Mirror Image choirs as they minister in prisons across the country. We have seen literally thousands of inmates come to know our Savior. As we travel in our buses, it never ceases to amaze me the number of billboards that adorn every highway. Most of them paint a picture and offer some type of invitation to participate in whatever it is they are offering to the public. It makes me reflect on my own life a great deal. Because of the privilege of being on television through The Encouraging Word broadcast ministry, I find myself being recognized in the most unlikely places and by the most unlikely people. Whether I feel like it or not, whether I am having a good day or not, I have a serious responsibility to love like the Lord Jesus. Every argument in the book can be used and every excuse can be made, but Jesus makes it abundantly clear when He connected our love for one another as a primary means by which "all men" will become connected to the heart of God.

You and I are living, walking billboards of God's grace, mercy, and love. Love is the primary means by which we are identified. This is the means by which they know who we are. It does mean I have to watch the way I talk to my wife, react to an inconsiderate person on the highway, deal with an inefficient waiter in the restaurant, issue a directive to a subordinate, respond to that man in the local church who truly believes God has placed him there to bring a personal word of discouragement every time the congregation meets to consider the business of the church, and so on. Tough order, to say the least. But Jesus said it. We must do it!

In other religions throughout the world, love is not the identifying banner or the evidence of faith. A number of these religions, in fact, focus more on trying to *find* love, to search it out. This is done through long spiritual journeys or completing certain works and various tasks which promise love, inner peace, and complete fulfillment. As Christians, we know that is simply not the case. True, inner peace will not be accomplished by means of saying this prayer or bowing in that direction. For Christians, the standard-bearer of our faith is love because God is love. Unfortunately, however, Christians are not always the stellar depiction of love in action. Oftentimes, we do not show love the way God would; we do not always see others through Christ's eyes.

I remember being invited to adjudicate a dispute in a church in Louisiana many years ago. Upon arrival, I found myself seated on the platform in a called church meeting. On one side of me sat the pastor and on the other side sat the chairman of deacons. Opening remarks were made, evidently designed to set the stage and invite all present to participate in an open forum. Without further ado, an individual stood and within the space of about one minute left no doubt about his opinion. The problem was not his opinion in the matter. It was the venomous spirit and the unkind manner with which he voiced his opinion. I quickly rose to my feet, reminded the people that I had been unanimously invited to adjudicate, and then proceeded to lay down some of the essential principles of conduct given to us by our Savior. I am pleased to tell you a semblance of order was restored despite the fact, but perhaps because of the fact, that the offending individual "stormed" out of the building. Ladies and gentlemen, we must be very careful in our conduct toward one another. I truly believe one of the many reasons why the Lord is not blessing some churches is because of this very fact.

Yet despite our inabilities, despite the fact that we *will* fall short, we must struggle daily to show love to others through our words and deeds. Remember friends, it's a race; it's about perseverance. Even when we mess up, even when we fail to love our brothers and sisters as we should, we should get up and keep running. Loving others must be our desire, our conviction. In all we do, we must seek to love others the way Christ loves the church, graciously and sincerely. He gave Himself over to death in order to show us love, Divine love, the kind of love that knows no limits.

2. Love is the window to our faith.

Now, I love this one, folks, even though it is particularly hard for me. As I reflect on its essential meaning, I hear the Lord Jesus saying, "Don Wilton, you are the window through which others see the love of God."

Now, that will tell you why this is so difficult! There have been a thousand times in my life when people have looked through the window of my life and have seen anything but the love of God. In my earlier years, I found this particularly challenging on the sports field. I guess I have always loved to do anything involving a ball. I particularly have loved playing ball with my three children. And, now, my daughter-in-law, Annabeth, loves sports as well. God is so good! It continues to give me much delight to beat my two grown sons, Rob and Greg, at golf (every now and then), or trounce my daughter, Shelley, in a game of basketball at the net perched outside our garage. My kids, of course, have a different opinion in these important life-and-death matters. The challenge for me, however, whether playing tennis, golf, badminton, lawn bowling, cricket, rugby, soccer, ping-pong, or my own version of Michael Jordan slam-dunk basketball, is that my competitive nature wants to win. Bad shots have never sat well with me. And sometimes, I have had to learn the hard way.

The straw that broke the camel's back for me came through the awful example of a fellow pastor many years ago. He was the sweetest man one could ever imagine when he occupied the pulpit in his church. But when we played golf together, he underwent a metamorphosis of some kind. To make matters worse, he was a scratch golfer, which, for those who know little about the game, meant that he was very good. Each Sunday he would stand in the pulpit and sweet talk his people while oozing with milk and honey. How good it was to just love everybody and show the love of Christ in such tangible ways to the community.

What he communicated on the golf course, however, was an entirely different matter. We stood on the first tee and "his highness" hit the ball slap down the middle of the first fairway. Best drive I had seen in years. Probably every bit of 280 yards! The problem was this man thought only a Tiger-like drive of 350 yards truly befitted a person of his caliber. Anything less was a failure. He snorted, huffed, and slammed his driver into the ground before beating a retreat back to the golf cart without so much as a thought for me, a fellow church member, and another man, who just happened to be a prospect for the Lord Jesus. By the time we arrived at about the fifth hole, it was all too much for me.

I want you to ask yourself a tough question. When people look at you, what do they see? Seriously, stop for a second and put yourself in your husband's shoes, your wife's shoes, or maybe look at yourself through the eyes of your children. What do they see when they look through your window? When God tells us to love our fellow Christians, it is because love is not only the standard-bearer of our faith, but love is the window of our faith.

We read earlier in John 13:35, *"By this all men will know that you are my disciples."* I think we often get this backward, though. Many Christians consider this to mean they ought to go out and love everybody in the world: Africa, China, India, and other places, but that is not exactly what God is saying. Rather, He is saying, "Yes, go and love everyone. Go to China. Go to India, but don't neglect those in your own backyard. Love those in your neighborhood, at your workplace, and in your home." Loving those around you signifies that you belong to God because through *your* window they see *His* love, which confirms who you are in the Lord Jesus Christ. In our efforts to show God's love to those around the world, we should be cautious not to neglect our own families, friends, and co-workers. After all, these people look into your window daily. They get to see the "real" us. So, ask yourself, "What is my window saying about Jesus Christ? What does my neighbor see when he walks by?" Perhaps this is why Jesus placed such emphasis on our neighbors. This is the Second Commandment. Perhaps He knew what we know and do. It is so much more comfortable to put all our time, energy, and money into the rest of the world, especially "those poor folks overseas." But what about the poor all around us? What about our own back doors?

This instruction from our Lord is not the same as the Great Commission we find recorded in Matthew's record of Jesus' final words before He ascended into heaven. Jesus said, *"All authority in heaven and on earth has been given to me. Therefore go and make disciples of all nations, baptizing them in the name of the Father and of the Son and of the Holy Spirit, and teaching them to obey everything I have commanded you. And surely I am with you always, to the very end of the age"* (Matthew 28:18–20). This mandate involves going, making, baptizing, and teaching. As critically important as this is, the Second Commandment to "love your neighbor" is a whole different ball of wax. Whereas the former pertains to our responsibility as believers to share the Good News with those who do not know it, the latter pertains to our behavioral disposition to love like Jesus. The old proverb, "charity begins at home," comes to mind. The first refers to our work; the second refers to our character. The Great Commission is a living testimony to what we do, whereas the command to love our neighbors is a living testimony to who we are. The first is a decision every Christian must make because we have received the love of God. The second is a mandate every Christian must follow because he is a disciple of God. The first is an inner choice based on the fact that Jesus died for all people, the latter an outward manifestation of an inner change; the first a presentation of the love of Christ to a lost and dying world, the latter a pronouncement of the salvation of a lost and dying person. The first is about sharing faith. The second is about demonstrating faith. Phew!

Have you ever had the pleasure of going to New York City during Christmas? It is absolutely spectacular! It is truly one of my favorite places to visit during that time of year. Karyn and I had such a delightful visit one year after accompanying Dr. Billy Graham to the United Nations. The magnificent tree in Rockefeller Center, the iceskaters buzzing around, the snow on the ground, the cool winter air, the choirs singing carols, and people from literally all over the world finishing their Christmas shopping make the experience almost magical. It is a vibrant, picturesque place to visit.

Over several decades, many now-famous storefront windows have been an attraction for visitors and spectators. Tourists, and many locals for that matter, will pass by and observe the glamorous, creative, and sometimes strange department store windows. Macy's, Bergdorf Goodman's, and Saks Fifth Avenue are just a few who participate in dressing their windows for the Christmas season. Now some of you who have never had the opportunity to see these in person may be thinking, "It's a window. How great can it be?" Well, let me tell you—people wait in long lines to see some of the more popular ones. The windows can be breathtaking. Upon first glance, you can clearly see the detail, effort, and time put into each display. The windows are thematic in nature. Some tell a story, others are thought provoking, and some are just plain pretty. Whatever the case, the windows of New York City are something not to be missed.

Now, because I'm not a big fan of standing in line in twenty-five-degree weather, I like to wait until the crowds have died down and look at the windows late at night. Personally, I think they are more beautiful in the moonlight than in the light of day anyway. Nevertheless, as we walk down the streets, holding our third cup of coffee from Starbucks in an attempt to keep warm, we peer into the windows. Some are wild and crazy, filled with bright colors and have seemingly nothing to do with the season at hand. Some leave me puzzled (it's those thought-provoking ones that you're not quite sure about what you're supposed to be provoked). Some take me back to my childhood with wonderful depictions of Christmas through the eyes of a child. And then there are some that make me wonder just how much time they put into decorating it. I mean, some of these windows can get really elaborate! But no matter what we find when we glance through the glass, we want to look. We want to see what's on the other side looking back at us.

Well, friends, when the pedestrians of your life are walking by, what do they see when they look into your window? Is it a depiction of self? Is it a picture that doesn't make any sense? Is it confusing or misleading?

Or do they see the love of God, plain and simple? Mark my words, people *will* look. They will glance over as they walk by or they will stop and linger. In any case, be ready because your faith is at stake. Love is the window by which others see our faith.

3. Love is the defining indicator of our faith.

Why must we love our fellow Christians? Not only because love is our evidence, not only because love is our window, but also because love is the defining indicator of our faith. In 1 John 3:14, the apostle puts it like this, *"We [those of us who profess to know Christ] know that we have passed from death to life, because we love our brothers."* We know that we are believers first and foremost. We know we have been forgiven of our sins. We know our names are written in God's book of life. Our faith is evident because we love our fellow Christians. Those people who claim to know Jesus Christ but have no love for fellow believers are abiding in death. They do not have the love of God in them. Luke 6:43–45, reads:

> *No good tree bears bad fruit, nor does a bad tree bear good fruit. Each tree is recognized by its own fruit. People do not pick figs from thornbushes, or grapes from briers. The good man brings good things out of the good stored up in his heart, and the evil man brings evil things out of the evil stored up in his heart. For out of the overflow of his heart his mouth speaks.*

You are not going to find an apple growing from a weed. It just won't happen. Apples come from trees—apple trees. Weeds come from, well, weeds. Likewise, you will not find love as an indicator of faith from someone who does not know God. In order to know real love, we have to experience it first. It is just what I was saying earlier in this chapter: we must know God to know love. If we know God and have a right and real relationship with Him, our hearts will be full. We won't have to think, "Okay, today I will have to love someone. I will do X, Y, and Z to show my love. That will do it." No. Love will be the outpouring of our hearts because it is what we have stored up. An apple will blossom from an apple tree because that's what was planted. Love will flow from our hearts because we are filled with God's Word. Our ability to love will indicate to others that a deeper, more sincere form of love exists. This love will be the indicator of our faith in Christ.

Moms and dads, I am going to pick on you for a moment. Maybe you are wondering whether your son or daughter knows Jesus Christ. Apply this litmus test. Ask yourself, "Does my son or daughter desire to be around fellow believers?" Stop and think. If you have to beg a person to come to church, to be involved with Christian people, to be involved in Christian activities, that person probably does not know Jesus Christ.

According to God's Word, loving fellow Christians is a key indicator of our faith. Those who have passed from death to life in Christ should also love their brothers and sisters in Christ. Take my relationship with Karyn, for example. She is, most certainly, the best thing that ever happened to me bar none! I would rather be with her than with anyone else in the world. I love being with my wife. The chairman of deacons doesn't have to hold a meeting and say, "We need to pass a resolution to ask our pastor if he would spend a little time with his wife." I am glad to report to you, and my wife will confirm everything I am telling you, that we gravitate toward each other. I want to be with her all the time. When I am gone, I feel like I have a hole in my heart. She is truly my best friend. We love to hang out together. We laugh together, cry together, go through valleys together, and climb mountains together. You do not have to beg me to be with my wife. I want to be with her. Why? Because I love her, that's why. And so it is when it comes to our relationship and attitude toward other Christians. Do you love being with other Christians? Do you love them in your heart and by your actions? Love is a defining indicator of our faith. Make sure that in your day-to-day living, your faith in the Lord Jesus Christ is defined by love.

We have discussed three reasons God places such a high emphasis on loving other Christians. Perhaps a deeper understanding might provoke further thought and action. To help us in this regard, I want to examine something very significant presented to us in Hebrews 13:1. I want to hone in a little on the word "love." The word for love used in verse 1 is actually "Philadelphia." As most everyone knows, Philadelphia is the city of "brotherly love." So, God is telling us to keep on "Philadephiaing" each other—Ha! Seriously, if you break that word up into its two components, we have "phileo" and "adelphos." The first part, "phileo," in the Greek text, means "deep and abiding affection." It speaks about a root affection, something that's grounded and runs deeply. The second part of that word is "adelphos," which literally means "kinsmen." When we are talking about brotherly love, we are talking about a deep, abiding affection for our brothers and sisters, a very special bond. God is saying that because we have a kinsman relationship together in Christ, we ought to love each other as kinsmen. If we are kinsmen, we need to understand two remarkable things.

1. We have the same Father.

We have the same Father. He is God, and He is none other than the God and Father of our Lord Jesus Christ. All believers, everywhere in the world, come from the same womb, the womb of God. We may live in different places, speak different languages, and have different skin colors but, as believers, we have the same Father, we are all brothers and sisters in Christ.

There are many times in life when this truism is particularly significant. Our prison population serves as a good example. As I said earlier, we have had the privilege of traveling to prisons of every shape and size all across America for many years. Together with these friends of mine,

I have spoken in maximum-security prisons, juvenile detention centers, women's facilities, and halfway houses of every description. Many times we hear the horrible tragedies and downright criminal activities of some of society's worst offenders, but few of us truly know the rest of the story. Our prisons are a seething mass of pitiful humanity, to say the least. I have stood and simply watched as the inmates pour out of their cell blocks all dressed alike and color coded according to the nature of each offense and the longevity of each sentence. There they come, old and young, single, married, and divorced. I have met medical doctors in prison, newspaper editors, teachers, lawyers, bricklayers, mothers, fathers, grandparents, sons, and daughters. Line upon line. Hot and sweaty, cold and alone. Some are as cocky as a parrot in a cage, some are as docile as an alligator taking a nap, some are as fierce looking as a wild animal with rabies, and some are as mellow as a baby on a mother's breast.

Most of my messages in these prisons revolve around similar themes. I tell the inmates of my own experiences around the world. By so doing, I take them on a quick journey outside the confines of their environment. This provides an opportunity to talk about the obvious. And that is the enormous diversity of the people of this world. Just think about it for a moment. From Australia to Africa, Europe to Japan, China to India, what a diverse and complex world we inhabit! A world filled with all kinds of people. Red and yellow, black and white. They are no different than you and me and no different from every prison population in America.

I am quick to point out, despite differences in appearance, language, culture, and creed, that all people have common needs. All people want to be prayed for. All people want to be respected. All people want to be loved. All people want to be forgiven. All people want to have a new beginning. All people want to have hope, not only today and tomorrow, but also beyond the grave.

What an opportunity to share the greatest news known to man.

What a heavenly Father we have! He is the One who prays for us. He is the One who gives us meaning and respect. He is the One who loves us despite ourselves. He is the One who makes us brand new. He is the One who gives us hope today and for eternity. Wow. What a Father! From one institution to the next we have been privileged to see thousands of desperate people come to place their faith and trust in our heavenly Father through His Son, the Lord Jesus Christ. It always brings to mind that most incredible statement of fact that, *"Therefore, if anyone is in Christ, he is a new creation; the old has gone, the new has come! All this is from God, who reconciled us to himself through Christ and gave us the ministry of reconciliation"* (2 Corinthians 5:17–18).

It all began when God gave His only begotten Son. While most people claim to know exactly what this means, many do not fully comprehend the immensity or the depth of what that entails for each and every one of us. We have no idea how great, how unbelievably spectacular it is to be seen by God as a sibling of the Lord Jesus Christ. You see, when God looks at me, He doesn't see Don Wilton with all the bruises, abrasions, and scars sin has left behind. Instead, He sees His Son, who by His sacrifice on the cross has made it possible for me to be covered and cleansed from my sin. As a result of this wonderful act, God sees perfection when He looks at me. Not because I am perfect, my wife can attest to that, but because Jesus Christ lives in me and *He* is perfect. His blood covers me. The theological term which more clearly describes this incredible act of God is "imputed righteousness." What this means simply is that once we have expressed our belief in Christ, once we have confessed with our mouths that He is Lord and believed in our hearts that God raised Him from the dead, we are declared righteous. So far, this sounds an awful lot like justification, but it goes a little bit deeper. Imputed righteousness is Christ's own righteousness imputed to the believer. It does not belong to or come from the believer himself; it is not through works so no man can boast. Rather, this righteousness is credited to the believer's account because Jesus took the debt of sin away once and for all.

Having the same Father, that is being brothers and sisters in Christ, means that we all came from the womb of God. Some people say, "The virgin birth is not important." On the contrary, the virgin birth is an absolute fundamental of the Christian faith! Why is the virgin birth so important? Because Jesus Christ did not come from the seed of a human father implanted into a woman. Jesus Christ was begotten of God. Now I want you to hold onto this: when we are "born again," we are born of the womb of God.

Nicodemus had a real problem with this whole concept of being "born again." He went to Jesus and asked, "Master, how can I come into your kingdom?" Jesus turned to him and said, "Nicodemus, you must be born again." Nicodemus said, "What! You mean I have to enter once again back into my mother's womb?" Jesus said, "No, that's not what it means—that is being born of water. To become a member of My kingdom and My family, you must be born of the spirit. You must be born of the womb of God!" When you are born of the womb of God, the Spirit of God rests upon you. God, by His Spirit, implants His seed into you, and you become reborn. That is what it means to be born again. God recreates you.

What does this mean for us as Christians? It means that all believers, from every descent, from every tongue, and from every nation, who have trusted Jesus Christ as their Savior, come from the same womb. That is why the Bible says, "One Lord, one faith, one baptism" (Ephesians 4:5). God has given us the authority to call one another brothers and sisters in Christ. This is a hard thing to understand, I know. Let's look at it like this. I have a beautiful daughter. She is my daughter, but I am telling you she is also my sister in Christ. I have two sons, but they are also my brothers. My sons and my daughter have been born of my seed, but they are also my brothers and sisters in Christ because they have trusted in Him. We have all been born of the seed of God, the womb of God—we come from the same place.

It is an amazing thing, folks, to know that we are brothers and sisters in Christ and with Christ. And it just keeps getting better. Here it is: the Father of our Lord Jesus Christ is also *our* heavenly Father. We have access to God, the Father, just the same as Jesus. Do you remember when the disciples came to Jesus and said, "Lord, teach us to pray."? What did Jesus say? He began, "Our Father . . ." Now, you might think, "What do you mean, 'Our Father'? What right do I have to pray, 'Our Father'? We're talking about God here! Can I really call Him Father?" Yes, you most certainly can! He is Abba, Papa, Daddy, and Father. Do you know why I can pray, "Our Father?" I have this privilege because I am born of the womb of God. He is my Father. He is your Father, and He is the Father of our Lord Jesus Christ. Amazing, isn't it? We all have the same Father. What does that make us? It makes us kinsmen; it makes us brothers and sisters in Christ.

So, we have established that we are all brothers and sisters in Christ, right? Well, if you are a parent of two or more children or grew up with siblings, you know that oftentimes, brothers and sisters will fight. It's almost a given. In the church, sitting in the pew beside you, is your sibling. Unfortunately, this kind of behavior has surfaced in the local church. The tragic truth is many will fight with a brother and sister in Christ as much as with a biological brother or sister. This causes many divisions in the church. Do you know how critical it is for a church body to be united? It is absolutely paramount. I want you to know that I boast only in Jesus Christ about my church body. People say to me all the time, "How can a church numbering in the thousands be so unified?" It is because it is God's mandate. He said that's the way it has to be in order for the body to work properly and effectively. It really is quite sad to hear about all the infighting that seems to go on in so many of our churches.

One of the greatest tragedies in American history was the Civil War. It pitted brother against brother and sister against sister. Many historians consider this chapter a blemish on the foundation of America. Others regard this as a stain on the incredible history of this incredible nation. How grateful we can be to be living in a day and age when so many broken fences have been restored. While there is still much to do, much has been put in place in an attempt to provide for a better future for all our citizens.

A greater dishonor happens when God's people fight against each other in the church. Some people believe it is not possible to have a church where people do not fall out of fellowship with each other. But it is. I have seen it work, even in my own pastoral charge. Impossible though it may seem, God has no limit on what He can accomplish with a congregation of believers who are truly united in Him. Some suggestions that may be helpful to you would include a clear understanding of the pastoral letters in which we frequently read about the importance of unity in the body. Then there must be a willingness on the part of the leadership to demonstrate unity in their own behavior. Unity starts at the top. It will never work, nor have any lasting effect on a congregation, when the leaders are bickering and jostling with one another for a seat at the right hand. Sadly, I have seen churches whose deacons or elders or leadership groups spend half their time in conflict with one another. And it is usually about power. The power to control what is done or not done. The power to have the final say so. The power of greed. And many times these power struggles are carried out in the name of the Lord Jesus. Surely this is an abomination! In reality, the only opinion that counts is not an opinion. It is our business only to know the mind of Christ, who is the head of the church. Nothing more and nothing less.

After this, unity must not only be taught and demonstrated, it also must be enforced. One of the reasons why the people in our church seldom get mad, upset, or bent out of shape in public is because we teach it, demonstrate it, and enforce it. One place to do this is in a new member orientation setting where the principles and practices of unity are clearly laid out while a definitive statement is made concerning the response to un-Christ-like behavior. Many evangelical churches in America today are fighting with one another in the house of God. People come to "business meetings" with bones to pick, pet peeves to sort through, and personal agendas to meet. We come down firmly on this issue. We will not act this way in the house of God! None of us have ownership over the body of Christ.

2. It is the absolute truth.

As kinsmen, we love each other because we have the same Father. In addition, we are to love each other because it is the absolute truth. Friends, love for other Christians is based on absolute truth, not personal preference or even personal convictions. We have no right to bring our personal preferences or personal convictions into the body of Christ. Understanding this and putting it into practice will help us love our brothers and sisters in Christ even when they are unlovable.

Personal preference is related to individual likes and dislikes. In recent years, choruses and praise teams are becoming more and more prevalent in modern worship styles. Some people love these catchy choruses while others hold to the old hymns of faith. Neither is wrong. It is simply a matter of personal preference. You, as a member of the body of Christ, have no right to bring your personal preference into the House of God to cause division.

Often, I hear of churches who part company because of things as trivial as what color carpet to put down or what color of paint to use on the walls. Have you ever heard of anything so childish? One church even went as far as painting one side of the sanctuary blue and the other side beige. The people who liked blue sat on one side and the people who liked beige sat on the other side. I'm serious with this, folks. You think I'm kidding, but some churches actually deal with matters such as these. The saddest part of this story is that they refused to speak to one another over something as ridiculous as the color of the walls! I can't, for the life of me, understand what makes some people think that the church is there to *only* serve them. It's like their personal preference of wall color is commandment number two of the Ten Commandments.

Some people try to rationalize their behavior by imposing their personal convictions on others. Personal convictions are based on the way you interpret God's Word. Some of the principles in God's Word are clear-cut, black and white. Some are not so clear. For example, many Christians are personally convicted that they should not go to the movies. Others are personally convicted that they should close their eyes when they pray. Some women are personally convicted that they should never be seen wearing pants or shorts. These things are not black and white in God's Word. You, as a part of the body of Christ, have no right to bring your personal convictions into the house of God with the intention to cause division. Individually, and as families, we should interpret God's Word using other Scripture references, prayer, and godly guidance. On some issues that are not clear and apparent, we will have varying personal convictions. This is all dictated by how we interpret God's Word and how the Holy Spirit directs us. Regardless, personal conviction is not a tool to mislead or manipulate the situation so that our own desires, wants, or opinions win out. Personal conviction should never be a method to change the opinions of others to fit our own. This is a misuse of God's Word.

God's Word is the absolute truth! The principles outlined in the Word of God are the principles that we have the right to bring into the House of God. God's Word says that some things are right and some things are wrong. As a part of the body of Christ, we must stand and support absolute truth. If we come together and agree in our churches, we will be able to love one another as brothers and sisters should. There will be no cause for division or hatred. Agreement based on absolute truth will always foster love and unity. Bottom line is I have done my best to teach my people the vast and essential differences between absolute truth, personal conviction, and personal preference. And I think most of us would agree a good understanding of these differences has had a tremendous impact on the life and ministry of our church and the way we relate to one another in the body of Christ.

Why Is Love Essential in the Body of Christ?

1. Because God Said It

The fundamental reason, the only reason, we need to love fellow believers is because God has made Himself very clear on this vital issue. It's right there in Hebrews 13:1, *"Keep on loving each other as brothers."* Any questions? Love is essential in the body of Christ because God said it is.

I feel so sad for churches that operate on man-made covenants. Such documents certainly have their place. They speak to the history of the church and define the functioning of the church in terms of some important issues related to government and so on. But we must be very careful that the covenant is totally subservient to the Lord Jesus Christ through His Word and not the other way around. Many fine churches have lapsed into apathetic comas, have become embroiled in controversies through personal disputes, and have literally shrunk to nothing because of the legalistic interpretations of a few diehards who place more value on the conclaves of their founding fathers than on the inerrant and infallible Word of the Living God! Somewhere in our churches across America, does somebody have the courage to stand up and say, "We will love each other because God said we should, period?" It is not a popularity contest. It is not to get points or win stars or receive awards; it is about following the Word of God. Loving others as brothers and sisters is what God commands us to do.

The sobering thing is many of our children and youth are watching us at work. All too often they see behavior unbecoming the child of God. Some churches almost go into armed rebellion over a simple request to purchase something for the young people or to enlarge the children's play area. These power struggles, in reality, are public demonstrations of how not to behave toward one another as believers. Should we really be that surprised when so many of our students take off to college and never darken the door of a church again? Some can't wait to get as far away as possible from the churches they grew up in because of the pitiful behavior of the grown-ups. If our love for one another as Christians begins to bleed down into our families, even America as a nation could be impacted positively.

One of the greatest gifts a mom and dad can give their children may surprise you. No, it is not a new car or even a good education (as important as this may well be). It is pure, old-fashioned, down-to-earth love for one another. Yep, I truly believe the greatest gift parents can give to their children is that mom and dad love each other. It has been well stated that you can give your children everything in the world, but if you don't love each other, your family will be in trouble. I have often said, with a twinkle in my eye, that if you really want to see a happy little face at home, then just let your child catch you in the kitchen hugging your child's mother. And, so it is in the context of the church. God can bring people together who are gifted beyond reason, but if they do not love one another, they will stay in conflict and all those wonderful gifts will be lost in the process; they will be in vain.

The same applies to the staff of a church, no matter how big or small. My staff and I are best friends inside and outside the confines of the church. We have seen this principle at work over many years of true love and friendship together. As a staff we are totally united in spirit and practice. We operate on a covenant together that centers on our love toward one another and our unity in heart and purpose. The golden thread of our covenant lies in our absolute loyalty to one another. We love together, serve the Lord Jesus together, work together, and prioritize our families together. I truly believe this is one of the greatest gifts we can give to the local church. Our people genuinely love to see the way in which we love one another as a staff. It's intentional. It's joyful! It's wonderful! It's significantly impactful, and it's most definitely biblical! Just think for a minute how many churches you know that are ripped apart by disloyal staff members who build their own little empires and are led by pastors who are insecure and shallow. No church like this will experience lasting growth.

2. Because It Is the Evidence of Conversion

The second reason love is essential is because it is the true mark of a Christian. It is a key indicator to whom we belong. The way I love fellow Christians tells me about the genuineness of my faith. As previously stated, loving others honestly is how the world will know we belong to Christ. You see, there is a special kind of love we share with others when Christ lives in us. It runs deep; it doesn't ask questions; it doesn't wait for recognition. This kind of love is not common in society today. A base form of human love that is not grounded in the essential character of God's love is oftentimes conditional and rewards-based. This kind of love seeks its own desires, its own lusts. Perhaps it is good to be reminded of the most quoted Scripture used by many a minister at wedding ceremonies. In 1 Corinthians 13:1–13, Paul puts this love in its rightful perspective:

> *If I speak in the tongues of men and of angels, but have not love, I am only a resounding gong or a clanging cymbal. If I have the gift of prophecy and can fathom all mysteries and all knowledge, and if I have a faith that can move mountains, but have not love, I am nothing. If I give all I possess to the poor and surrender my body to the flames, but have not love, I gain nothing. Love is patient, love is kind. It does not envy, it does not boast, it is not proud. It is not rude, it is not self-seeking, it is not easily angered, it keeps no record of wrongs. Love does not delight in evil but rejoices with the truth. It always protects, always trusts, always hopes, always perseveres. Love never fails. But where there are prophecies, they will cease; where there are tongues, they will be stilled; where there is knowledge, it will pass away. For we know*

in part and we prophesy in part, but when perfection comes, the imperfect disappears. When I was a child, I talked like a child, I thought like a child, I reasoned like a child. When I became a man, I put childish ways behind me. Now we see but a poor reflection as in a mirror; then we shall see face to face. Now I know in part; then I shall know fully, even as I am fully known. And now these three remain: faith, hope and love. But the greatest of these is love.

Wow! What a list! What a demonstration of Christian faith!

3. Because It Is an Essential Witness

The third reason love for fellow Christians is essential is that it is our greatest witness. One of the ways we try to share the good news about the Lord Jesus with our community is with a wonderful program known as Faith Evangelism Strategy through the Sunday school. We have numerous people on our list to visit. On one occasion, a group of our faithful people went out to visit a family with the goal of sharing their faith with them. One can only imagine the joy when both the husband and wife came to know Jesus Christ and were baptized. Shortly thereafter, their brother came to know Christ and was baptized. Now watch what happened next. These three people went out and invited their parents to our church. Do you see the trickle-down effect? We have a "New Friends Dinner" hosted by various families in our church. These dinners are informal and are designed for those who are interested in joining our church fellowship. You talk about an act of love! My wife and I join the other staff and have fellowship together with our new friends. On this particular occasion, the parents of these new Christians came to the New Friends Dinner. At the end of the dinner, Scott Stancil, our minister to adults, went over to the man whose name was Leo Zybd, and said to him, "Leo, have you come to the point in your life that if you were to die you know you would go to heaven?" Leo looked at Scott and said, "Scott, I am a truck driver, and I've already had two terrible wrecks. I drive a big rig with oil in it." He said, "I don't know how I've survived, but, no sir, I don't know that I'd go to heaven." Scott led Leo to the Lord Jesus Christ right there in the home of other fellow Christians. A few weeks later, Leo was tragically killed in a truck accident before he was to be baptized the next Sunday morning. We were all so saddened by this event, and our hearts went out to his family. But think about it. Today he is in heaven all because of some precious people who loved each other with such passion that it became an action.

Friend, how about you? Are you part of the family of God? Are you my brother or sister in the Lord Jesus Christ? I pray so. If you have accepted Him as personal Lord and Savior, I ask you this: Are you ready to run? Are your tennis shoes laced up and ready to go, or are they sitting on the shelf covered in dust? As Christians, we must put love into action; we must be ready, willing, and able to run the race with love.

Love is an action word; it's a verb. It requires that we *do* something. I challenge you to open yourself up, put on your running shoes, and allow God to use you. He wants to show us a love like we have never known before. And He wants us to show that same love to others. But in order to do this, we must see the world and the people living in it through the eyes of Christ. In order to love like Jesus, we must begin to see others the way Christ sees us—without fault, without judgment, without guilt, without limits.

THE FOURTH CHAPTER

A Kingdom Plan

It is not what we say about our blessings, but how we use them.
This is the true measure of our Thanksgiving.

—*W. T. Purkiser*

Scripture Reference: Hebrews 13:2
Do not forget to entertain strangers, for by so doing
some people have entertained angels without knowing it.

I want to begin this chapter by asking you a very simple question. What are blessings? Seriously, take a second and think about what that word means to you. Is it a cliché? Is it corny? Is it a "churchy" word? Has it become so commonly used in today's society that the true meaning has been obscured? I certainly hope not. I hope that when you think about what a blessing is or what blessings you have in your life, your heart grows a little warmer and your eyes grow a little brighter.

When I am asked to examine such a word, I think of all the gifts I have been given: my lovely wife, my beautiful daughter, my two handsome sons, a wonderful daughter-in-law, my gracious church, my loving friends, my dedicated co-workers, my health, and my home. These people, these things are all blessings to me. God put them in my care; He gave them to me as gifts. God's blessings are all around us. The life we have been given is filled with them. They are literally in everything we see, touch, taste, smell, and hear. What are blessings? They are everything—from the smallest speck of hope to the grandest display of affection, blessings are everywhere. You see, we come into this world naked, hungry, and helpless. It is because of the kindness and goodness of God that we are clothed, fed, and guided. God does not owe us this and we do not deserve this. It is simply because of His grace and through His love that we receive these wonderful gifts. God the Father gives good gifts to His children every single day. It is up to us to notice them, take care of them, cherish them, and thank Him.

My dear friends, all of us are blessed in many ways. I'm certainly a blessed man! But unfortunately there are those individuals who look at life and can't see their blessings; they fail to notice what God has given them. We all know these people. We might even *be* these people. They are the "glass-half-empty" folks. They say things like, "Well, yes, I know I have my health, but my hand aches from time to time and I just don't think there's any hope of it ever getting better." Because they choose to focus on what's "wrong" in their life, they miss out on all that's "right." Instead of highlighting their other blessings, they dwell on this *one* problem. The "half-empty" folks have allowed themselves to be consumed by negativity; their joy has been robbed. Beyond this group, there is another collection of folks whose glasses are not only half-empty but apparently have a hole in the bottom, too. They say, "Yes, I know I have my health, but my hand aches from time to time and I don't think there's any hope of it ever getting better. I just don't know why God is allowing such awful things to happen to me. Nothing's ever going to change." To be quite honest, these folks take the life right out of me. I walk away thinking, "Man, I'm beat. They have worn me out!" The leaky, half-empty perspective truly breaks my heart because they miss out on God's blessings. They are so consumed with self that they fail to recognize God at work all around them. Friends, I'm a blessed man. This is *not* because God has given me more things or better things or an easier time in life, but because God has given—period. I recognize that I deserve nothing, am entitled to nothing, and every good and perfect gift I have is because God has made it so. I look at everything I have as a gift from God.

If you see yourself in one of these two aforementioned categories, I encourage you to look around, listen to the news, and travel to other parts of the world. Come with me to Baghdad, and you will soon understand the blessings we have been given here in America. Speak to one of our heroes in uniform who have served in Afghanistan, and you will begin to appreciate your blessings. It is so important to bear in mind that God provides us our daily bread. He will always make sure we have everything we need for every day we're on this earth. Beyond that, any further gift is just icing on the cake!

Remember the manna God sent down from heaven for the Israelites to eat each morning? In Exodus 16, we read how God saw to their needs by providing food for them every day. Their instructions were to take only what was needed for that day and trust that God would again provide them with food on the following morning. And do you recall what happened? They tried to store up more than their share, more than a day's worth of food. God caused the manna to spoil and smell. He would not allow the food to be kept overnight because the people had to learn to trust Him. In the same way He provided manna for the Israelites, He provides us with blessings; He meets our needs. Now the "glass-half-empty" and the "glass-half-empty-with-a-hole-in-the-bottom" folks would have looked at the manna and said, "Is this all we get? Where's the ketchup? And can I get something cold to drink with this?" They would have totally missed the point; they would have missed God.

God gave manna to the Israelites in order to provide them with their "daily bread" (literally, folks). In addition to meeting our physical, tangible needs by giving us blessings like our homes, cars, food, and money, God has given us mercies new for each day. He sees to it that we will not be put under that which we cannot bear. In Lamentations 3:22–25, God's Word says:

Because of the LORD's great love we are not consumed, for his com-
passions never fail. They are new every morning; great is your
faithfulness. I say to myself, "The LORD is my portion; therefore I
will wait for him." The LORD is good to those whose hope is in
him, to the one who seeks him.

God's blessings, the gifts He gives us, are just what we need. He
knows when we need a little more and when we need a little less. As parents, we do not buy our thirteen-year-old daughter the same present we
buy for our three-year-old son. That would be crazy. Our daughter
would look at us like we had completely lost our minds. Can you imagine the scene? It's Christmas morning and the three-year-old opens up
his monster truck set. It has all the bells and whistles anyone could possibly want. It has lights, it makes noise, and it is so cool! He is in hog
heaven! Now, it's the daughter's turn. With great anticipation, she un-
wraps her present and, that's right, she got a monster truck set too. No
expression, no words, nothing—she is completely silent. Heaven only
knows what she must be thinking, right? There isn't a parent on earth
who would ever intentionally do this to his or her children. We know
our children. We know what they want and, more importantly in this
case, we know what they don't want. In the same way and on a much
deeper level God knows us. He knows what we need to make it through
each and every day. His compassions, His mercies are new every morning for Don Wilton, for Karyn Wilton, for Sally Sue, and for John Doe.

God bestows countless blessings on us in the form of tangible gifts.
But He doesn't stop there. He gives us the abilities to make it through
life by providing unyielding mercies and daily compassions. His gifts,
His blessings cover us. He takes care of our physical hunger as well as
our spiritual hunger. The Bible often talks about the fact that man cannot live by bread alone. The blessings we can touch and the blessings we
can experience are linked; they are not mutually exclusive from one another. Everything we have comes from God—everything! It is evident

that blessings are not only the objects we can wrap our hands around, but they include our families, friends, and those we have yet to encounter. Blessings can be the experiences we have, the journeys we take, and the emotional ties we make along the way. Obviously, being blessed goes way beyond material possessions. Being blessed is the state of our hearts. As Christians, we have all been blessed richly and undeservedly. And I think (if you'll beg my pardon while I play the role of God here) that God, who is our Father, is up in heaven saying, "Children, share your toys with your brothers and sisters. Share the gifts I have given you with others."

If we are willing to open our eyes and look around us, we will see those in need of a shared blessing. I believe wholeheartedly that God directs our paths so that they will cross with those who are in need. Just as God meets our physical and spiritual needs through blessings and gifts, we can do the same for others. Maybe we need to share a kind word or show compassion. Maybe we need to give them money or assist in a physical matter. In either case, God has a purpose, a "Kingdom Plan." But before we are able to share our blessings with others, before we can tap into His Kingdom Plan, we must have a heart that recognizes our own blessings. This "glass-half-empty" stuff is not going to help anybody. It's like that old saying, "Don't look a gift horse in the mouth." When you question the value of a gift or long for something better, you are cheapening the gift, devaluing the giver. In order to put into action the directive found in Hebrews 13:2, *"Do not forget to entertain strangers,"* we have to stop focusing on what's wrong and underline all that's right. There are so many opportunities in life to share our toys, to share our blessings with a lost and dying world. If we are alert and ready, we will become increasingly aware of the needs around us. As a result, we will love like Jesus and become part of God's Kingdom Plan.

I had the occasion to experience this many times while I was at the New Orleans Baptist Theological Seminary. One time in particular will stand out in my mind forever. It was a Friday night. We called some friends of ours and suggested we get together for an evening of fun and fellowship. It was rather late in the evening when we determined to go out and stock up on some "good" junk food. So, my friend and I went out to a local grocery store near the seminary. As we stood in line to pay for our food, I noticed a couple standing at the checkout next to us with a small child. The little girl looked to be about two years old and was standing with what appeared to be her mother and father. The mother was holding the little girl very closely. The father stood beside them clutching change in one hand. In the other hand, he held a small carton of milk and a package of powdered sugar doughnuts, the kind one buys that can also be used as doorstops! The couple stood staring at the floor, the little girl was quiet and still, unlike any two year old I had ever seen before. As I looked at them, trying not to be obvious, God deeply touched my heart. Through my subtle glances, I noticed the sad, hopeless looks on their faces. I could not keep my eyes off of them. As we made our purchase and left the store, God strongly impressed on my heart to give them all the money I had in my pocket. As we walked back to the car with our junk food, I stopped dead in my tracks. I looked at my friend and said, "I'm going back into the store and give that couple all the money I have left in my pocket." My friend looked at me and said, "I was thinking the same thing." We quickly pooled our money and surprisingly had about $200 between us (I had completely forgotten I had gone to the bank that day to get some cash for the weekend.) After we gathered the money, I quickly walked back into the store, hoping they were still there. They were next in line so I hurriedly walked around behind the man. In my South African accent I said, "I have a gift for you; please don't turn around. A friend and I want you to take this cash simply because we love the Lord Jesus Christ. If you don't know the Lord Jesus Christ as your Savior, find someone who can tell you about Him; it will be the greatest thing you have ever done." The man allowed me to slip the rolled-up wad of cash into his hand, and I noticed a tear begin to stream down his right cheek. I left as abruptly as

I had entered. We never faced each other. I never gave him a chance to say anything to me. My friend and I quickly left and we never expected to see the man or his family again, although I must say we seemed to enjoy our junk food more than usual.

God had blessed me in my early days of seminary, and now it was my turn to be a blessing to someone else. No recognition, no glory, and nothing in return. Simply the satisfaction of knowing I was completely obedient to God's prompting in my heart was all I needed. Now was that man an angel? Did I have the opportunity to entertain angels unaware? Was my wife going to kill me because I gave away all of our money? I think not (on my account), but I do believe he was part of God's overall Kingdom Plan.

I do not tell that story to brag about what I did, but simply to illustrate what God is saying in these verses. Share your blessings! Listen to Him when He prompts you to lend a hand. He has blessed you for a reason, and He has a Kingdom Plan in store for you. He wants you to be a part of it by sharing what you have with those with whom you come into contact.

Years went by, and I soon forgot about that man and his family . . . until one day. Being a professor at the seminary meant that I also was invited to preach from time to time in the services held on Tuesdays, Wednesdays, and Thursdays of every week of the semester. On one occasion, I was invited to preach during the first week of the new term. As was customary, students, faculty, and others in attendance who wanted to greet the chapel preacher would line up to shake hands and offer various sentiments to the one who had just preached. This was always a special time of interaction and fellowship. On this occasion, when they were all gone, I noticed a well-dressed gentleman standing to the side, anxiously waiting to talk with me. As he approached me with his hand outstretched, he asked, "Dr. Wilton, may I share a story with you?" I said, "Certainly, I would love to hear your story."

As he began to talk, tears cascaded down his face. He said, "Ten years ago, I had no job, no money, no food, no home, and no hope. My wife and I saw no way out of the situation we were in, and therefore made a suicide pact. We had a two-year-old daughter who was starving and sickly because I could not provide for her. We were living in an old car that would barely run and, so, we decided to do the unthinkable. Our plan was to drive to New Orleans, find a bridge or high building, and jump off it, taking our daughter with us. The last thing we wanted was for our little princess to have to live in a world that had been so cruel to her mother and me. We planned to take our daughter with us because there would be no one left to take care of her. We loved her so much and could not stand to see her suffer any longer. My wife, who could not bear the thought of our daughter dying with no food in her belly, begged me to scrape a few dollars together so that we could at least go into the grocery store of the parking lot we had ended up in and buy whatever we could for her to eat. And, so, I scrounged around in my pockets and in the car for money and finally got enough change to buy a small carton of milk and some white powdered doughnuts. As we were standing in line to pay for what we believed would be our daughter's last meal, a man walked up behind me, thrust a roll of money into my hand, and said, "If you don't know the Lord Jesus Christ, find someone who can tell you about Him; it will be the greatest thing you have ever done." Before I could even turn around, he was gone. When I looked down, I was astonished to see nearly $200 rolled up in my hand.

"That man's generosity rocked our world. My wife and I sat in the parking lot of that store all night long, weeping uncontrollably while trying to decide what to do. As the sun came up, we knew what to do. With a full tank of gas, we headed back up the interstate toward Hattiesburg, Meridian, Tuscaloosa, and on to the tri-cities area of Alabama where we had come from. I found a job at a food store and gradually our lives came back together. Some weeks later, my wife, my daughter, and I heard some gospel singing as we strolled past a small church on a Sunday morning. It was like a magnet to me. I couldn't help myself. I had to go inside. As we sat awkwardly in the back seat, the minister began to speak of the love and forgiveness of God in the Lord Jesus Christ. My heart opened and I remembered what had been said to me in a parking lot in New Orleans, Louisiana. Dr. Wilton, today is my first day of classes at this seminary. God has called me to preach the gospel. I have wondered about that man for over ten years and today, when I heard you preaching in chapel, I recognized your accent. I recognized your voice, and I knew that man was you."

Shall I utter those words again? Share your blessings. Share your blessings. It doesn't matter what you have to give; it doesn't matter if you think it's silly or inconsequential. Listen to the promptings of the Holy Spirit and share your blessings. God has an intricate Kingdom Plan designed for us. But it is up to us to go where God is, to be where He is working. We must pay attention when He prods and obey when He speaks. Our blessings are gifts from God. Sharing with those who might be in desperate need of a kind word, a wad of cash, or an ear to listen will keep us running on the right track. We only have to find out what He wants us to do, and then do it! Put the words of Hebrews into action; put on our running shoes and run. There are three principles God would have us hide in our hearts regarding our blessings:

Principle #1—Share your blessings intentionally.

At the beginning of verse 2, the writer says, "Do not forget." Notice that is an imperative, not merely a suggestion. It is a mandate from God. He is looking into the heart of a person like me and saying, "Don Wilton, I'm about to lower the boom on you, son. I'm about to tell you that because you have been blessed, do not forget to share your blessings intentionally." And, so, I began to examine this: "Lord, why are we exhorted to not forget?" What causes people like me to forget? Let me make a number of suggestions to you as to why we are prone to forget to share our blessings intentionally.

I believe that selfishness is the main culprit. All of us are intrinsically very selfish people. I do not know if you've ever met a person about whom you would say, "Goodness me, they are so tightfisted!" May I just paraphrase what you are saying there? "Man, they are selfish. They don't seem to want to share their time or their money with anyone." Let's be honest, folks. A tightfisted person is a selfish person, and all of us struggle with that because it is our human, endemic nature to put self first. It is my basic nature to want to do things for me: I want to look right; I want to feel right; I want to take care of number one. It is a human trait, is it not? Our natural propensity in our endemic nature is to be selfish, to try and direct the attention toward ourselves. This selfishness causes us to forget. Because we are so focused on self, we can easily lose sight of the needs and desires of others.

We know that being selfish causes us to forget, but so does being blind. People today, including me, spend many hours walking around like mules with blinders on. Some of us even take it one step further by putting patches directly over our eyes. We think, "If I don't see it, it doesn't exist." Have you ever experienced this with a small child? I bet you have played peek-a-boo at least once in your life. They cover their eyes and think that because they cannot see you, you are not there. It's the same thing with adults. In some cases, we intentionally choose to be blind—we just don't want to know what's on the other side of those blinders. In other cases, we turn a blind eye to the situation—we see what's happening but choose to do nothing about it. In the Gospel of Matthew, there are numerous instances where Jesus is interrupted along His journeys. (Now, I know He would never put it quite like that, but the truth of the matter was that oftentimes, His path was redirected because someone needed Him. And you know what? He didn't mind one bit.) In Matthew and on into Mark, we read wonderful accounts of healings: a woman reaching out for Jesus' cloak in a feeble attempt to be cured of her infirmity; a ruler kneeling down in front of the Savior begging for his daughter to be raised from the dead; a man bringing his paralytic friend to Jesus' side in hopes of a miraculous healing. In a crowd of people, no matter where Jesus went, He was constantly bombarded with pleading, begging, and bargaining. He could have just walked on by and said, "I can't heal your daughter today, ma'am. I'm late for a lunch meeting with My disciples." It's almost comical to think of Jesus saying something like that. It just wouldn't happen. My Jesus would never turn a blind eye to someone asking for His help—never!

Now, unlike us, Jesus had the luxury of knowing at first glance what the need was. Though in many cases He would ask, "What can I do for you?" He gave us the perfect example of how to be alert and notice the needs of others simply by asking. He never turned a blind eye to the crowds, to the paralytics, to the blind, to the mute, or to the children. Why would Jesus do this? Why would He have to have conversations with the disciples, saying, "Slow down, guys. I'm not finished here yet"? Why would Jesus have to tell them, "It's okay, bring the little children to me. We have time"? It is because Jesus understood that blindness in the human heart prevents us from sharing the blessings God has given us. It is a great deterrent to giving. Sometimes, we merely shut if off. We do not want to see them. It is easy to be blind when it comes to all the things that are going on in the fabric of society. Blindness will most assuredly cause us to forget to share our blessings intentionally.

I'm afraid I do not like this next one, because it is so true of me. We forget to share because we're forgetful. "What did he just say?" you might be asking. What I am saying is that sometimes we simply forget to share with others. Often this is exacerbated by being too busy or in a hurry. Whatever the case, whether you didn't leave yourself a Post-It note to remind yourself or you were distracted by a new project, the outcome remains the same—we forget. Unintentionally, albeit, we still forget. The old adage "out of sight, out of mind" is so true in this regard. And awfully convenient, too.

I consider myself a young(ish) man, but already it amazes me the number of times I forget to do something. Fellow staff members in my church will come up to me on a regular basis and say, "Now, Pastor, don't forget, you said you were going to . . ." Recently, I was reminded of this; my forgetfulness was brought to my attention. I was getting ready for work one morning and I slipped on my sports coat. I reached into my pocket to straighten it out and grabbed hold of a piece of paper. As I opened the paper, I suddenly remembered what it was. Several weeks prior, a precious church member handed it to me and said, "Pastor, please read this when you get a second." Well, I felt terrible. I couldn't believe I had stuck the paper in my pocket and completely forgotten about it. On many occasions, members of my congregation will hand me slips of paper and say, "Pastor, would you take this and read it later? It is very dear to my heart." And I say, "Certainly, I will." And I do take it. I put it in my pocket with every intention of reading it later in the day. And most times I do. Well, on this particular occasion, I didn't. I forgot to look at this important prayer request from a dedicated church member. What a wonderful pastor I am, right? None of us are exempt from the curse of forgetfulness. We all forget at the best and the worst of times. Despite our efforts, despite the Post-It notes, and despite the e-mail reminders, some things still creep past us in life. We will let our loved ones down. We will forget to share our blessings.

Now, I'm sure there is somebody out there who may read this book and look at me quite rightfully and say, "Pastor, you can talk all you want to, big boy, but you've got no walk." I hope when you read about my inconsistencies that you also hear my heart. I don't want to forget, but sometimes, to be honest, I do. I simply forget from time to time. I don't just go home and automatically put myself up against the wall and pat myself down. I'll tell you what I do when I go home, folks. I get out of my suit as quickly as I can, put on flip-flops, and throw on my shorts. I had someone come to my door one day and say, "Pastor, you wear jeans!" I said, "Rooty, toot, toot, yes I do!" I am as normal as the man next door!

But I am forgetful—just like you. I am human and sometimes I forget. Admitting that we are guilty of this does not dismiss us from the wrongdoing. If anything, it should make us more aware, more sensitive to the fact that sometimes things will slip by us. We need to be watchful and on guard so we do not forget.

We have established thus far that we neglect to share our blessings because we are selfish, we are blind, and because we forget. The fourth reason I believe we fail to share with others is because we are disdainful. Most of us, including myself, develop a disdain, a disregard for the needs of others. There have been times in my life when I have gone to a restaurant or my family and I are on vacation, and a person comes up and has a need. In my heart, I have a feeling of disdain swelling up. In my heart, I think, "Just go away; I would like to be with my family now. I don't want to deal with this while we are eating dinner." Recently, at the end of an exhausting day, I went to the hospital to visit a very sick church member. It was already past nine in the evening. As I walked back to my car, a woman ran across the parking lot calling my name. I stopped and the woman began to share her story with me. She told me that her husband was very near death with terminal cancer. For many months, he had watched *The Encouraging Word* live television broadcast on Sunday mornings. I had become his "pastor." She said, "Dr. Wilton, it would mean so much to him if he could meet you. Could you possibly go back into the hospital and visit him? Could you pray with him?" My heart sank. All I really wanted to do was go home, eat dinner, and see my family. I said, "No, I'm so sorry, but I cannot go tonight. I will come back tomorrow and see him then. How does that sound?" I could clearly see the disappointment flood her face. She kindly replied, "I understand. I know you are very busy. Thank you, anyway." As she turned to walk back toward the hospital, I said, "No, wait! I'm sorry. I will go with you."

I knew exactly what God would have me do; there was simply no question. I had barely spoken the words, "No, I'm so sor . . ." when my heart said, "Don, you are going to march straight to that hospital room and pray with that precious man!" My heart knew, but my head was stubborn. She and I made our way to her husband's bedside. When he looked up and saw us standing there, his eyes lit up. He said, "Dr. Wilton, I cannot believe you came to see me!" As I sat and talked with that couple, I shared the blessing of time, prayer, and fellowship with a dying man. I cannot explain this, but I was the one who really received the blessing that night. I was so close to disobeying the nudge of the Holy Spirit. I just wanted to go home and eat my pot roast. Thankfully, God pushed, He prodded, and I listened. Despite my disregard, I didn't miss out on an opportunity to share. And my pot roast never tasted better!

Just recently, I ran headlong into someone who had a very severe handicap. I came to quickly understand that the only way this person could communicate with her family was by virtue of a computer. I discovered this person had a computer that was six years old and, on top of that, it was mostly broken. I'm sure you can appreciate how six-year-old computers function. I mean, computers change and evolve so swiftly that it's hard to keep up with the technology. Computer years are like dog years—they move quickly. So, if this computer was six years old, that would make it more like forty-two (sounds jolly young to me, but for a computer it is far from ideal). Anyway, I said to the person telling me about this young lady, "Please go and tell her right now that she'll have a new computer by Monday." He said, "How do you know that?" I said, "Let me tell you, beginning with me, I know lots of people who would be willing to buy her a new computer today!" This girl *had* a need (I'm happy to report that her need was met), and in my eyes it was easy to meet it. Sometimes it's easy to spot the need, know exactly what to do, and do it without hesitation. Just like with this girl. She needed a new computer to help her talk to her family. This is not rocket science. And such needs are all around us.

Why do we fail to share our blessings? Maybe it is selfishness; maybe it's blindness; it could be forgetfulness or disdainfulness, but what about fullness? Have you ever thought about that? We forget to share because we are full. When my wife and I go grocery shopping, she always makes sure I have been well fed before I go with her (I like this arrangement so I am not complaining!). You see, she knows if I do the shopping on an empty stomach, I will come back with five loads of stuff, and it will most likely have more junk food than wholesome food. There is something interesting about having a full tummy that causes us to forget what it means to be hungry. When I grocery shop and my belly is full, I am less likely to come back with highly nutritious items like popcorn, chips, cookies, ice cream, chocolate-covered peanuts, and a host of other delicious things.

I always have plenty of food. Consequently, I have difficulty genuinely understanding the meaning of hunger. Likewise, I do not have a true understanding of what it's like to be truly and painfully cold in the winter. Except when I was in the Army, of course. But that was years ago. The passing of time is a great healer. It is also a great eliminator. It's amazing how quickly we forget how it once was. A friend of mine, who has done rather well in the business world, made a comment to me recently. He said, "You know, Don, I am so glad you reminded me of my growing-up years when we had nothing. I guess I have gotten used to the blessings I have today."

Sounds familiar, doesn't it? I'm going to go out on a limb here and say that most of us have never faced this reality. Many of us just do not see the cold people out there. I mean, if we're cold, we grab a jacket or sweater, find a blanket, turn on the heat, and get some hot chocolate— that makes it all better; problem solved. So many of the problems that are out there are exactly that—out there! We watch it out there on television all the time. It's always someone else's backyard, and we like it that way. Those poor Indians in India. Those poor babies in Africa, starving and all that. Even in our own towns, most of us seldom have to drive through the poor areas of town. We just avoid them. It's really as simple as that. In America, most of us have the ability to keep ourselves warm. Stay cold? Come on, how can anybody possibly get cold in America? But I tell you, God looks into my heart and says to me, "Don Wilton, do not fail to share your blessings because you are full! I have given to you so you can share with others. There are those who get cold. Give them a warm place to lay their heads." How do we give it? We give it intentionally. It is a deliberate act of choice. We must not fail to share our blessings intentionally.

One of the best things our church does is through the Helping Ministries Center. Wonderful people devote their time and energy, as well as their money, to this intentional endeavor to give to those in need. It brings to mind the Lord's admonition to begin our service of giving to others in our own backyard. I believe He called His backyard Jerusalem. Think of it like a large pool of water. Drop a pebble in the middle then watch the concentric circles develop in an ever-expanding outward movement to Judea, Samaria, and then to the outermost parts of the world. This mandate spoke to a deliberate action. Intentionality in giving is critical to the success of giving. I've heard moving stories of families who devote an entire Thanksgiving to real-life action. Some ideas include serving meals at a rescue mission, going to a prison to share a little love, delivering groceries to the poor, and even just driving around looking for someone to help. It's amazing what needs there are out there, and it is wonderful to experience the joy of intentional giving. Just do some random acts of kindness for a change. It will change your life!

Principle #2—Share your blessings outwardly.

"Do not forget to entertain strangers." This is an interesting principle. Notwithstanding the fact God tells us to love one another, we also need to love all those who are not directly considered to be "one another." In other words, we are to share our blessings with strangers. You know whom I am talking about. It is those people who fall outside our circles of comfort.

In Paul's time, hospitality was considered one of the greatest virtues of all. Hospitality is the act of recognizing our blessings and then sharing them outwardly with others. When I share outwardly, it is an opportunity for me to express my gratitude and thankfulness for the many blessings God has given me. I can minister to others through my blessings, and I can give God all the glory. The gift and expression of hospitality is a wonderful testimony to the One who has given it all to begin with.

When God tells us to share outwardly, He is telling us to reach outside our comfort zones. Let me ask you a searching question. When was the last time you and your family took someone out to eat who was not a part of your inner circle? How many times do you go out and intentionally reach outwardly? Do you always sit with the same person, or do you go and talk to other people? Do you make others feel at home? It seems to me sometimes that God looks into my heart and says, "Don Wilton, it's time to share your gifts out loud." We must run the race which is set before us by loving those with whom we come into contact, those we know and love and those we have only just encountered. In order to put God's Word into practice, we have to open our hearts up to strangers, "For by doing so we have entertained angels without knowing it." Share your gifts outwardly.

I have often thought how incredible it would be if every member of our church took someone different out to lunch each Sunday. This can be organized easily on a systematic basis. Can you just imagine the impact this would have on the average fellowship?

Principle #3—Share your blessings unknowingly.

God exhorts us to share intentionally, to share outwardly, and to share unknowingly. To share unknowingly speaks to the motive for which I share. This causes me to examine my heart before God in order to make certain I am sharing with a pure motive. When I share, I should not be asking for anything in return. Giving with strings attached happens much too often in our society today. We need to stop this nonsense as Christians. Give intentionally and specifically because God has told you to give, but give with a pure motive. Take your hands off and say, "I am giving this because God put it in my heart to do so. I have no control over it once I hand it over." He will bless that.

If a beggar comes to your door and you give him money for food with a pure motive, you gave it unknowingly. So what if that beggar goes and spends the money you gave him on alcohol? I pray that he does not, but my motive must be right in order for God to bless it. What the beggar does or does not do is out of my hands. I remember hearing a knock on our door some years ago. A pitiful man presented himself to me and accompanied his pitiful look with an even more pitiful story. His whole life was a wreck. He was hungry and desperately needed help. My wife made him a sandwich and spiced it up with an assortment of goodies. The man pleaded with me for money for train fare and whatever, but I felt the food was sufficient at the time. After he had left our home, I went outside to discover he had unceremoniously dumped the meal on the sidewalk. Did this make me mad? Most certainly!

But I cannot give and control every time I give. I must give simply because God has blessed me. Period! We give without strings attached; we give without the compulsion to control the outcome. If he says, "I need bus fare," and I give him money for that, I need to do so with a pure heart—no strings. If he wants to go and abuse my generosity, I still need to give it to him unknowingly. Do you ever get abused when you give with a pure heart? You'd better believe it, but give with motives that please the Lord anyway. Now the unknowing part of giving ought never to be an excuse for stupidity in giving. Let's be really clear about this. My son, Greg, learned this lesson in a big way. He and my son, Rob, and daughter-in-law, Annabeth, live in New Orleans as they prepare for the ministry to which God has called them. They have established a most unbelievable ministry in that city under the direction of Ignite Mission. In an effort to reach the students of New Orleans, they have devised several component ministries like HIMNI and Out of Range, among others. Needless to say, I am so grateful to the Lord for giving me children who have such a passion to serve our Savior, and I am so grateful for the way in which they are being used to preach and teach the Word of God around the country.

Into this picture comes Greg. A bigger heart you cannot find. A passion for the down and out. A God-given hunger to reach the helpless and homeless. Some time ago, his generous heart led him to "offer" his car to some gentleman who was being ministered to on the campus of the New Orleans Seminary. What began as a simple act of generosity quickly turned into a nightmare. Bye-bye car! The man took off in Greg's pride and joy. He disappeared into the swamps. Greg's generosity and desire to give unknowingly cost him big time. I mean no more car to drive. And the car his Mom and Dad had bought him on top of it. The news, however, is good. I truly believe the Lord answered our prayers and understood Greg's Christ-like motive in giving. With the help of a wonderful pastor from the neighborhood and the New Orleans police, the man who had originally taken off in Greg's car was tracked down, and then the crack cocaine dealer who had "rented" the car from the original for a sample of "crack" was tracked down. Instead of being broken into small parts in Austin, Texas, for immediate shipment to India or someplace, Greg's car was retrieved (with a big sigh of relief from Greg). I do believe Greg has learned the essence of unknowing generosity. It is better, sometimes, to just simply give the man a ride rather than giving him the very means by which he came to be in the predicament to begin with. "Loaning" such a man a nice car was simply "too great a temptation." And you can imagine how much mileage we have gotten out of this! Giving unknowingly not only speaks to the motive for which I share, but it speaks to the manner with which I share. If I give unknowingly, it demonstrates *why* I am giving and *how*

I am giving. I have been guilty over the years of giving with this hand then demanding certain behaviors or things in return with the other hand. God wants me to give simply because He puts it in my heart to do so. He wants me to give with a pure motive, and He wants me to do it in the right manner. God desires for us to give in a spirit of spiritual excellence. This means that I need to give way beyond normalcy. I have to look outside myself in order to give to others the way God wants me to. I need to give excellently, magnificently; I need to give hilariously!

Did you know the original Greek text of 2 Corinthians 9:6–7 quite literally could be translated, "God loves a *hilarious* giver." I want to look at this text for a second. Let's read these verses in context, *But this I say: He who sows sparingly will also reap sparingly, and he who sows bountifully will also reap bountifully. So let each one give as he purposes in his heart, not grudgingly or of necessity; for God loves a cheerful giver* (NKJV). When I read these verses, I am compelled to ask myself, "Don, am I a cheerful giver, or do I give grudgingly or out of necessity?" I want you to ask yourself the same questions. Do we give little drips and drabs of our resources to others? Do we give because we feel obligated? Or are we giving open-handedly, without asking for anything in return and without strings attached? When we give of our homes, time, money, and talents, we must do so with an open, pure, and cheerful heart. We need to simply say, "Lord, here I am; use me. I want to give hilariously!"

Have you ever given something to someone and it made you content just to do so? That's what God is talking about in these verses. We aren't to give out of necessity or because we have to. We are to give because we want to; because it is what makes us truly happy. If we are believers in Christ and followers of His Word, giving to others will make us happy; it will bring us joy. When my children were growing up, I loved to buy games and toys for them. It didn't matter how much we spent—if it came from one of those quarter machines or if we had just dropped fifty bucks on a Christmas present, it was all the same to them. (We could have probably saved a lot of money if we had shopped more from the quarter machines, huh?). At any rate, they were always so sweet and precious to watch as we gave them a new book, a sticker, or a special piece of candy. It made my day giving my son a piece of gum that was too big for his mouth. You know, one of those brightly colored gumballs that were horrible for his teeth. His eyes would light up, he would rub his hands together in anticipation, and then he would chew it all day long. Something so little made him so happy. And, because I knew it would be the highlight of his day, I gladly gave him the chewing gum (well, as often as my wife would allow it, anyway).

Having a pure motive, a willing heart, and a cheerful attitude to share our blessings with others will lead to manna falling from heaven each day of our lives. God's Word says that He will provide us with His mercies new for each day. It says that we are not to worry about tomorrow because tomorrow has enough of its own worries. We should only be concerned with today. So give your gifts, give your time, and give your money. The Bible tells us that when we share our blessings, we just might find we are entertaining angels without knowing it. When we give, God's manna will pour out of heaven. The more you open your hand and let go of your gifts, the more God will put in your hand. Remember what happened when the Israelites tried to store up their food? It spoiled. It is just the same with our blessings—we must share them with others and not store them up for ourselves because they will surely spoil and ruin.

I had a dear lady come and see me recently. She is not a member of my church and lives quite a long way from the church. She is an older widow who has lived alone for many years. I felt like I was sitting in the presence of an angel. Ironically, her name was Grace, and as she began to talk to me, I thought about the grace of God. She told me what a blessing this church had been to her through the years. She was not able to go to church and felt like I was her pastor. She asked me if I would be so kind to preach her funeral one day. I told her I would be honored. As she was leaving, she said, "Pastor, I am giving what I have to the television ministry, *The Encouraging Word*, because it has been such a blessing to me." I could not help but think about the manna of God. We have been a blessing to this woman, and now she is a blessing to us. We give without question, and God overwhelms us every time!

Over forty years ago, a small group of men and their wives from my church got together, and God spoke to their hearts about something. They pooled their money and resources and made an investment in something. They had no concept of what God would do with a television ministry at their church, but they knew they wanted to share their church with others. I believe, to the glory of God, you could parade hundreds of thousands of people right through our church doors who have been blessed because a small group of people made an intentional decision to share their blessings. Today we are privileged to be hearing life-changing testimonies from fifty states! And it all began with a small group of committed and unselfish people fifty years ago.

Do you know what can happen in twenty-five years if we open our hands up to God right now? You and I can't even begin to comprehend the great promised land that awaits us. God will multiply our gifts and talents to an extent we can't even fathom. If we are willing to put our blessings to work for God, who knows what He can do? God longs to perform great and mighty acts in us and through us. We just have to be willing to share. The more we open our hands to God, the more He is going to fill them up. It's time to share the blessings, folks. It's time for us to open our hands and release whatever it is that we are holding on to. God cannot use a tight-fisted person. Share your blessings, share your gifts, then sit back and watch what the power of God working through you can do!

In Matthew 25:14–30, Jesus tells the parable of the talents. In this story, He explains that a master went away on a long journey and left his servants in charge of his property. Before he left on his journey, he divvied out the talents as he saw fit (which, by the way, a talent is worth more than a thousand dollars). To the first servant he gave five talents, to the second servant he gave two talents, and to the third servant he gave one talent. The Scripture says, *". . . each according to his ability."* So, off the master went, and the servants were left to do as they wanted with their talents. The first servant, who was given five talents, put his money to work and doubled it. The second servant, who was given two talents, also put his money to work and gained two more. The third and final servant, who was given one talent, *"went off, dug a hole in the ground and hid his master's money."* When the master returned, he met with each of the servants to see what they had done with their talents. With the first and second servants, the master said, "You have been faithful in handling this small amount, so now I will give you many more responsibilities." Then the man who had buried the talents came to him and said:

> *"'Master,' he said, 'I knew that you are a hard man, harvesting where you have not sown and gathering where you have not scattered seed. So I was afraid and went out and hid your talent in the ground. See, here is what belongs to you.' His master replied, 'You wicked, lazy servant! So you knew that I harvest where I have not sown and gather where I have not scattered seed? Well, then, you should have put my money on deposit with the bankers, so that when I returned I would have received it back with interest. Take the talent from him and give it to the one who has the ten talents. For everyone who has will be given more, and he will have an abundance. Whoever does not have, even what he has will be taken from him.'"*

What we have been given by God, our talents and our gifts must be doubled, multiplied. God has given to us so that we might share with others. He has given us everything we have, from the air we breathe, to the water we drink, to the manna we eat, and to the mercies that are new each morning. We do not own any of these things—we are merely put in charge of them. Do not take for granted what He has done for you by neglecting to share your blessings with all those around you. Put the directive of Hebrews 13:2, into practice, *"Do not forget to entertain strangers, for by so doing some people have entertained angels without knowing it."* Keep running the race with perseverance; keep investing your time and money in others. *"Let us not become weary in doing good, for at the proper time we will reap a harvest if we do not give up"* (Galatians 6:9).

THE FIFTH CHAPTER

To Walk in Your Shoes

"He jests at scars that never felt a wound."

—*William Shakespeare*

Scripture Reference: Hebrews 13:3
*Remember those in prison as if you were their fellow prisoners,
and those who are mistreated as if you yourselves were suffering.*

I remember many years ago we had a banquet in our dining hall at church. My oldest son, who was fourteen at the time, was playing basketball in the gymnasium. During the banquet, a man quietly slipped in and whispered in my ear, "Rob has been hurt in the gym. You need to come quickly!" My wife and I got up immediately and rushed to his side. When we arrived, my son was sitting there in the middle of the basketball court with a crowd huddled around him. As we approached, it was obvious his arm was broken because the bone was literally bulging through the skin.

Friend, *I* had not broken my arm that day; *I* wasn't the one sitting on the cold gym floor. But the pain I carried in my heart as a daddy was almost too much for me to bear. It might as well have been my arm that was broken, my bone that was exposed, because my heart was aching desperately. You see, the pain I felt for my son ran the gamut. It was multidimensional. First, I was obviously aware of Rob's pain. I could clearly see that he was hurting. Second, I could imagine how he must have felt; my own arm began to ache. Finally, I was bent on doing anything I could to make it better, to alleviate his pain. In those first few moments, I experienced an array of emotions: sympathy, empathy, and compassion. And this is exactly what Hebrews 13:3 is prompting us to do with others.

Let's break down these three emotions to discern their similarities and differences as we seek to understand how we can put this command into practice. First, we have sympathy. According to *Merriam-Webster's Collegiate Dictionary,* sympathy is a tool generally implemented to share in another's pain or suffering. The essence of sympathy in action is that a person's feelings reflect or are like those of another. Simply put, sympathy is saying, "I realize you are in pain, and I'm so sorry for you."

Empathy is defined as "the action of understanding, being aware of, being sensitive to, and vicariously experiencing the feelings, thoughts, and experience of another of either the past or present without having the feelings, thoughts, and experience fully communicated in an objectively explicit manner." Empathy is best described by the old adage, "You've got to walk a mile in another man's shoes." Simply put, empathy is saying, "I can feel your pain though I've never experienced your circumstances."

Compassion is defined as "a sympathetic consciousness of others' distress together with a desire to alleviate it." In my personal opinion, compassion is the most mature, most evolved emotion of the three because it not only identifies with the sufferer in both thought and feeling, but it signifies action as well. It connotes an awareness of another's feelings coupled with the motivation and desire to change it. Simply put, compassion is saying, "I will do anything I can to remove your pain."

Why is it relevant for us to decipher between feelings of sympathy, empathy, and compassion? Why is it important to know how to implement these tools and techniques in our lives? It is as such because God's Word commands us to be sensitive to the circumstances and feelings of others, "to remember those in prison as if you were their fellow prisoners, and those who are mistreated as if you yourselves are suffering." Though it isn't imperative to be able to readily distinguish between these three emotions, it is helpful. It allows us a better understanding, a deeper awareness of those around us so that we can carry out verse three in our own lives. How do we affiliate with prisoners if we've never been in jail? How do we relate to those who are mistreated if we have never been in that situation? We do this by implementing sympathy, empathy, and compassion, undergirded by love.

In Hebrews 13:3, the author uses a prison and those who have been treated unfairly to illustrate his point. I suppose some who take issues quite literally may say, "If I want to fully identify with an alcoholic, then I need to go out and get drunk." No, that is not what God is saying. I can assure you that God's Word is not telling us to go to the local bar and turn up a few just to understand what alcoholics go through. It isn't necessary for us to experience each and every detail of another man's life in order to understand him or appreciate his circumstances. We can derive a good perception and realization of another's situation by being empathetic.

I am going to confess to you that I have a little more understanding of the prison parallel than some of you might think. (Big scoop on Don Wilton coming up—are you ready?) I spent one night in the brig when I was in the Army, and so did two hundred of my fellow soldiers. (Okay, not really that big.) I was a member of the armored division, and we had been to the movies. The paratroopers showed up at the same movie and started to tell us that they were better than we were. Everyone knows if you are a member of the airborne, you never tell a tanker that you are better than he is! So, all the armored division stood up, me included, and we decided to teach the paratroopers a thing or two. The military police didn't like that very much, so they stormed in, blew their whistles, and arrested the whole lot of us. We were thrown into the paddy wagon, and off to the brig we went. Despite the one night I spent in the brig, I do not have a true appreciation for what it must be like to live there. I have never been divorced, so how can I identify with people who have gone through a divorce? I have never been truly hungry, so how can I identify with the hungry?

It is, quite honestly, irrelevant if we have walked down the exact path as someone else in order to be able to get what they are saying. We can listen; we can put ourselves in their shoes; we can imagine what it might feel like to be in their situation. As Paul says in 1 Corinthians 9:22, in order to become all things to all people so that some may be saved, we must begin by listening to others—taking the time to really hear what they have to say. We must not be self-centered when we listen; we must not have an agenda or be thinking about our response. Instead, we must listen with compassion and understanding. You don't have to go get drunk to know what that feels like the morning after. You don't have to be beaten to know it hurts. You don't have to be divorced to understand that it devastates. We could go on and on with these sorts of examples, but the bottom line here is that God tells me to identify with prisoners and sufferers. Allow me to share three ways to make this possible:

1. We must remember them.

This one is pretty straightforward but often quite challenging to implement. It is so easy to forget people who are in need. Many of us lead busy lives. I know I do. I often find myself racing from one thing to another. People talking, decisions being made, opinions sought, places to be, and appointments to keep. Soon enough they become like ghosts passing by on a dark and foggy night. I can see their faces, but not clearly. I can hear their voices, but not distinctively. I can watch the tears streaming down their forlorn faces, but not completely. They stand in lines, long lines. They wait and hope. They watch and listen. They reach out and want to be touched. But we are not there for them. We've forgotten them. We've moved on. Another appointment. Another place to be. Another face to observe. Another story to hear. Another promise to make. I know this to be true because I am guilty, too. It is easy to forget that there are those who are suffering because they do not have what they need.

Christmas is such a wonderful time of the year and gives a great example of this dilemma. We are all well meaning and, at best, our motives are right. Just think about all we do and become involved in. There are angel trees, shoeboxes, parties, fund-raisers, volunteering, and displays of goodwill everywhere one can possibly imagine. The joy bells ring forth, the eggnog flows, gifts are exchanged, and much love between families and friends is shared. It really is heartwarming to see all the kind acts which are shown during the Christmas season. But how soon we forget that the needs we strive to address during the holidays continue throughout the year!

The same kind of "forgetfulness" happened when the tsunami hit Asia. It happened after 9/11. It happened after Hurricane Katrina. I have even heard people say that the hardest thing about the death of a loved one is not necessarily the immediate hole in the heart. It's not the time between the death and the funeral. Many find themselves in a fog during this time anyway. People I know and minister to often comment on the overwhelming outpouring of love and support they receive in those dark and difficult days when the reality of what has happened is still fresh. The problem, it seems, pertains to the days, months and even years after the separation has taken place. I'm told these are the loneliest of times. This is when depression can set in and take root. This is the time when people feel abandoned. This is why we have to remember that some needs don't go away just because time has passed. We have to make it a priority to think of those who are suffering and not forget to give.

2. We must identify with them.

You might ask, "Why should I identify with people in prison?" or "How can I identify with people in prison?" Let me present two points of identification:

We can identify with them because we have sinned too. I think that is really the point the author of Hebrews is trying to make here. Prison in those times was a little different from what it is now. Take, for example, an event that occurred in the courts of America in May 2006. Many people in America were horrified when Al-Qaida conspirator Zacarias Moussaoui escaped the death penalty as a jury decided he deserved life in prison instead for his role in the bloodiest terrorist attack in U. S. history. Newspaper headlines across the country read something like this: "MOUSSAOUI GETS LIFE IN PRISON: 'America, you lost!' Al-Qaida conspirator taunts afterward." This, however, is one of the many things that separates the United States of America from many other countries in the world. Due process is a vital part of our constitution.

This was certainly not the case in the times of the early church. There was no due process; there was no stellar legal defense team. You could be thrown in jail because someone didn't like the things you said. Period. However, there was still the same stigma associated with prison as there is now—it's not a great place to be. Paul, who seems to have been the author of Hebrews, was imprisoned many times. He had a thorough understanding of what a jail cell felt like, and he wanted others to know, too. Why? I think it's because he wanted to highlight, once again, that we are all on the same team; we are all brothers and sisters in Christ. It was his way of leveling the playing field, so to speak.

In most of Paul's writings, he articulates over and over that we are all the same in the eyes of God. We have all sinned; we have all fallen short. No matter how hard we try, we can't "win" God's favor. Using prison as a point of reference here allows the writer to say, "See, we are all the same. We all have a thorn in our flesh to struggle with; we all make mistakes; we are all in the desperate need of the grace of God!"

I mentioned earlier that I have had the privilege of speaking in prisons across America with incredible groups of students called Mirror Image as well as an equally wonderful group of senior adults called Yesterday's Teens. We've seen it all, really. I cannot adequately describe what it means to see hundreds of incarcerated individuals lining up in rows, walking with their hands behind their backs or in shackles. The looks on their faces are difficult to describe. There is a sadness, a lostness, a hopelessness etched, it would seem, into the faces of every offender. One incident will always stand out in my mind. We found ourselves in a maximum-security adult prison on the East Coast. Just getting through security was a feat within itself. We were all searched bodily and scrutinized thoroughly. The venue for the presentation was a gymnasium of sorts that had a stage area and a balcony that could only be accessed from the side entrance. Guards were everywhere, and tensions ran high. Eventually the officers began to bring the inmates inside. They came in categories highlighted by the colors of their fatigues. They were as silent as a night without a breeze and sat down in their assigned seats with expressionless faces. Just when we thought the place was packed to capacity, the side door to the balcony opened and another entirely different category of offenders were led in. The difference was they were all chained up. They had chains around their ankles, waists, and wrists.

The truth is you and I are as guilty as any prisoner in jail today! Sin is sin in the eyes of God. It is man who places the hierarchy on sin. In our society, it's easy to look down on someone who has committed a heinous murder and say, "Boy, he sure is bad. Just look at what he did!" Do you realize that any sin is a heinous sin against God? Let me put this in perspective. Murder, lying, adultery, stealing, cheating on your taxes, lust, shall I continue? *Any* sin we commit is all the same to God. That's hard to wrap our minds around sometimes. We are conditioned, accustomed to using society's standards to dictate the bad from the really bad (and we all know that society is usually not the best yardstick to measure right and wrong anyway). Let's just imagine for a moment what it would be like if we used God's standard for sending someone to prison.

We would all be locked up for sure! "Oh, no, I just coveted my neighbor's car. I guess I'm off to jail." "Oh, boy, I just told my girlfriend that I couldn't go to the movies with her because I have to work late. It's really because I have Panthers' tickets—it's off to jail for me." You see, the Bible says, *All have sinned and fallen short of the glory of God* (Romans 3:23). We can identify with prisoners because we have all sinned.

Furthermore, we can identify with prisoners because they are behind bars. We all know what it is like to be behind bars, at least emotionally if nothing else. Something we have not done, our inadequacies, or our behaviors have caused us to feel as though we are behind bars. Addictions, habits, or even the actions of others may cause us to feel imprisoned. Breaking free from the past is a difficult thing to do. Nevertheless, we can identify with prisoners because all of us have felt imprisoned at some point in our lives.

We can identify with them because they are lonely too. All of us identify with loneliness to greater or lesser degrees. Many are lonely even in crowds of people. Some are lonely because of the death of a loved one. Others are lonely because of divorce or separation. We can identify with prisoners because, at one time or another, we have experienced loneliness, too. We know what it's like when we feel forgotten, left out. Can you imagine what most prisoners must go through on a day-to-day basis being locked away from their friends, families, jobs, and lives? How lonely and depressing that must be.

Feeling forgotten is probably a very common emotion among prisoners. But we can still identify with, to some extent, what it's like to have been forgotten. Maybe you have experienced a tragedy or a loss in your life. At first, people flock to comfort you, but after a few weeks, the calls become fewer and fewer. After a month or so, you feel totally forgotten, alone. The pain is still there, but people go on with their lives. We can identify with people in prison because we, too, have been forgotten.

3. You must bear with them.

How can I bear the burden of another when I have not been through the same experience? Let me explain. Both of my sons love basketball. I can identify with that. I know about traveling, setting picks, and shooting lay-ups. My daughter loves to sing and has a beautiful voice. I, on the other hand, do not. I can't carry a tune in a bucket. However, I love my daughter and want to share in her passions, even if they don't come naturally to me. God, by His grace, endows me with this capability. And it doesn't have to stop there. I can apply that same philosophy with others. You and I are capable of bearing one another's burdens, joys, and sorrows. We just have to look beyond ourselves and take the time to peer into the hearts and minds of others. There are three ways we can do this effectively and efficiently:

We can be there in person. We can do something about it ourselves. If I am going to identify with sufferers, the first thing I can do is be there in person, reaching out to those who are imprisoned, who are sick, or those who have lost a loved one. There are those around you who are suffering. Open your eyes and go to them. Be sympathetic to their needs though you might not be able to fully understand how they feel. Sometimes all you need to do is be there, and sometimes you will need to meet their physical needs. Providing a meal, taking care of their children, or even cleaning their house are all actions that show love. Many times, we don't know how to respond when others are suffering. But I would rather take a chance on being there and not be needed than to be needed and not be there!

Recently, one of the missionaries who came out of our church had a tragedy in his family. He and his wife, along with their three children, hiked two miles into rugged terrain to a waterfall in the country they were serving. Their eight-year-old son fell thirty feet off a cliff overlooking the waterfall. John had to carry his son two miles on his back, get on a trail, and travel several miles before getting him to a hospital.

The boy died the next day. As John's pastor, I wanted desperately to be there in person, but it was impossible. They were on the other side of the world. A week later, they came to the United States and I *could* be there in person. Many of their friends were there in person to help and comfort them. After their son died, they wanted to be home with fellow Christians. They needed for their friends and family to be there in person.

We can send someone else in person. We may not always be able to be there in person, but we can play a part by sending someone else. As the pastor of a large church, I can't be with every member when they have a burden, but I can send someone in my place. I can send another staff member or a layperson to help bear the burden. You cannot be everything to everyone all the time, but you can have a part in helping others by sending someone else in person.

We can pray for them in person. What a wonderful gift God has given to us. If we want to identify with those in need, one thing we can certainly do to communicate this is to pray for them. Often, I will pray with people in person who are suffering or who have a burden. Occasionally, however, I cannot be with that person. But these days, through modern technology, I am afforded the opportunity to reach people almost anytime and almost anywhere in the world. With a click of a mouse, I can e-mail a prayer around the world. Through my cell phone, I can reach others and offer up a prayer for them. There is just something special about praying for people in their presence. It gives them the confidence they need to make it through their day. Sometimes all a person needs to hear is, "Let me say a prayer for you right now." Praying for others during their suffering often brings peace and comfort in a supernatural way.

Friends, I want to bring it home here. I want to put it as simply as I can. If you want to follow the instructions in verse 3, you must begin by loving one another. As it is written in John 13:34–35, *"A new command I give you: Love one another. As I have loved you, so you must love one another. By this all men will know that you are my disciples, if you love one another."* Being a sympathetic listener, having an empathetic heart, and communicating compassion with our actions will convey love to our brothers and sisters in Christ. Following the words of Hebrews 13:3 simply gets back to the basics: Love one another. If we have love, the rest will come naturally. Why do you think it hurt me so badly when my son broke his arm? Was it because I'm such a jolly good pastor? Nope. Was it because I'm such a good person? Nope. It's because I love my son. Period. It is only natural for me to hurt when he hurts, cry when he cries, and rejoice when he's happy. If we love one another, we will remember those who are mistreated, imprisoned and suffering. On our journey to the finish line, let's not forget to put into practice what we have learned here in verse 3, *Remember those in prison as if you were their fellow prisoners, and those who are mistreated as if you yourselves are suffering.*

THE SIXTH CHAPTER

To Love, Honor, and Cherish

"Recent studies reveal that 50–60% of married men and 45–55% of married women engage in extramarital sex at some time or another during their relationship."
—Atwood & Schwartz, 2002, Journal of Couples and Relationship Therapy

Scripture Reference: Hebrews 13:4
Marriage should be honored by all, and the marriage bed kept pure,
for God will judge the adulterer and all the sexually immoral.

There is part of me that wishes I could simply leapfrog over this chapter and just skip right over this verse in Hebrews. As a pastor and as your friend, however, I am not afforded that luxury. The Scriptures are clear on these issues and what I am to do regarding them. The Bible instructs me to tackle these sorts of matters head-on. But I will tell you, before I wrote this chapter I had a serious conversation with the Lord: "Now, Lord, do I really need to write about this subject? It is uncomfortable and some people might feel alienated. Lord, I want to address the subject of infidelity, but I want it to be well-received. Please bless the words I'm about to write. Let them be Your words and not mine. Dear Lord, help me as I write to be clear and compassionate. Help me be sensitive as I communicate Your will regarding marriage." And just as I suspected, God had a plan for me. He had a plan for this chapter.

Through my thoughts and prayers, the Lord Jesus Christ wrote something upon my heart that I simply must share with you. I pray that as we delve into this matter, our hearts will be open and ready to receive what He has in store for us. Whether infidelity has affected you directly or indirectly, most everyone has felt the influences at one time or another and is in need of help.

I love being a pastor. It is such a privilege and an undeserved honor. Precious people surround people like me, and they come from every walk of life. I love preaching the Word of God, and I love interacting with the whole perspective of life itself. But I cannot tell you just how difficult it is to love people and yet comply with the Lord's mandates concerning the laws that govern our behavior. It is one thing to talk about ethics in the workplace, attitudes on the job, and even real tough things like personality disorders that need major adjusting to Christlikeness, but it is entirely another thing to deal with immorality of this nature. Human sexuality adorns the billboards of life, but personal sexuality remains one of the untouchables. The only time sexual immorality is given the green light for public display is when it provides society with a juicy piece of gossip to chew on, even more so in the church of God.

There have, sadly, been numerous occasions when I have been called on or invited to referee conflict and heartache brought on by marital infidelity. In general, guilty parties usually react in two ways. Some become immediately defensive, arrogant, and retaliatory. The blame game begins, and some even resort to the most unkind tactics imaginable. I have sat and listened to once-loving husbands (or wives, as the case may be) openly chide their once-loved spouses by pointing to every conceivable sexual malfunction known to man. These outbursts include name-calling and even the most horridly unkind personal accusations about the partner's sexual inadequacies, failures, and limitations. I've heard it all from, "You have never given yourself to me," to "I can't stand the sight of you," to "You're boring in bed," to

"From the day of our wedding, I have never been satisfied by you." My heart has ached for the victim of this kind of defensive posturing that is only designed to justify what God calls sin. I do not believe there is ever any justification for sexual infidelity in marriage, whatsoever!

Gladly, however, I do want to report that some become immediately contrite before God and the one they have let down so terribly. Their faces speak a thousand words. A genuine humility surfaces, and repentance toward our Savior and toward their spouse is set in motion. Words like "I have sinned," "I cannot believe what I have done," and "Would you ever find it in your heart to forgive me?" begin to pour out of the mouth of such a one as this.

Fifteen years ago, I had a very good friend whom I will call Joe. I knew him well. He and his wife had precious twins—the cutest little butterballs you have ever seen! One day, word came to me that Joe was developing a potentially serious relationship with another woman. The word was that he had not done anything physical yet, but the relationship was certainly headed in that direction. I'm sad to say, he was a pastor of a church and this woman was one of his church members. So four of his friends who knew him and loved him got into the car and paid him a visit.

As long as I live, I will not forget that meeting. The four of us were anxious, saddened, and desperate for answers as we set out to confront our friend. A confrontation of this nature and this magnitude is never a comfortable or easy thing. But there we were—on our way to talk to our friend because we loved him and cared about his future. We drove to his house, rang the bell, and went in. We all knew what we were there to do, so we sat down and reasoned with him. I remember looking at Joe and saying to him, "Joe, let me tell you what you are about to do. You are about to throw away your wife, your children, your grandchildren, your reputation, your character, your friends, your community, your trust, and your integrity. You are about to throw away every blessing that you have been given and for what? I am begging you to draw a line, get a grip. Please, Joe, repent to your wife, repent to God, and stop this thing now before it goes too far." Sad to say, but that man, our good friend, scorned us to our faces. He did not draw a line; he did not confess. And I'm sure you know how the rest of the story goes.

Many years later, I saw him briefly. He is no longer a minister of the gospel. He had the marks of sin all over his face and looked like a very old man. I said to him, "Joe, what are you doing now?" He replied, "Oh, I work for a small company as a salesman." I asked about his children, and he said, "Well, to be honest, I haven't seen them in nine years." (He had not seen them in nine years! I cannot imagine being separated from my children for nine years!) After that, he turned to me and he said, "Don, I am begging God to do something here, but the silence is deafening. I don't know what to do or where to go. I feel like I've lost everything." You see, friends, the decisions Joe made early in life had destroyed the rest of his life. A few fleeting moments of fun, adventure, and intrigue left him broken and alone. I'm left to wonder, "What did he actually believe was going to happen with this relationship? I mean, where did he think it was going? Was he going to run off with this woman, get married, and live happily ever after? Seriously, what was his plan here? I guess that's part of the problem—he had no plan. He acted on his impulses, quite like children who lack impulse control. And now, years later, he is still paying for those poor decisions he made nine years ago.

Judging by the many people I have known over the years, consequences seldom are fully in focus when lust is at work. Some people call it "the heat of the moment," but it all adds up to the same thing. Sin has consequences. Bad consequences. And for the person who throws it all away for a few moments of passion, the consequences can be catastrophic. It's like the aftermath of a hurricane or a tornado. The warnings are always there. The storm is coming. The winds are blowing. Then it hits. And after it hits, it leaves a trail of devastation and destruction that includes children, parents, integrity, character, leadership, home, unborn grandchildren, and a ruined testimony for the Lord Jesus Christ. The list goes on.

The Bible says, *Marriage should be honored by all* (Hebrews 13:4). But according to our society, marriage has become pedestrian—dull and ordinary. As a matter of fact, just recently a story was published in *ESPN, The Magazine* about an NBA athlete whose wife had deemed him a "restricted free agent" one day a year. Now, some of you might be asking, "What in the world does that mean—a restricted free agent?" Well, this man's wife made a determination that one day a year he was allowed to go out and *be* with any woman he wanted, but just for that one day a year (or so goes her attempt at justifying this to herself). This couple bought a lie. She convinced herself that if she allowed him this one day, then he would not be tempted later when out on the road traveling with his team. Sounds like they both honor and cherish marriage a great deal, doesn't it? This is just one instance that illuminates how little society values marriage. I mean, look at Hollywood; consider the actions of some of the past presidents of the United States of America. Marriage is not taken seriously; it is not valued; it is not honored. So why all the fuss on my part? Why do I care if the institution of marriage is honored? I care because it is important to God. The Bible is clear about God's ideals on marriage. According to the Scriptures, there are three basic reasons for marriage, three explanations as to why God prioritizes the institution of marriage and why we should, too.

Reason #1: To have children

Think about our precious children. They are absolutely the apples of our eyes, God's special gifts. The Bible says in Genesis 1:22 and again in 1:28 (NKJV), *"Be fruitful and multiply."* Procreation is God's intended purpose. He said, "I am allowing you to get married, and will possibly give you the blessing of children." Why did I add the word "possibly" there? Let me explain. The Bible does not say that bearing children is a prerequisite to being blessed in marriage. In fact, I believe God deliberately chooses that some people do not have children. Consider my good friends, Chuck and Rhonda Kelley. Chuck is the president of the New Orleans Baptist Theological Seminary. They are the most incredible parents to scores of boys and girls each year. God has given to them imminent gifts of grace, mercy, and hospitality. They are not distracted by the needs of their own children. God has given to them an extraordinary marriage. He has not chosen to give them children because He had a different purpose for their lives. For many of us, however, one of the purposes of our marriage is to have children.

I truly believe this was one of the reasons God brought Karyn and me together as man and wife in 1976. While I could write a book on all the other reasons, I also certainly could write a book on the joy of bringing up our sons and daughter in this world. We have more fun together than one could ever imagine. The Lord has allowed us to travel the world and to view the entire world as God's parish. We have also hurt together and cried together. We have made many mistakes and have achieved great things. Today, my daughter is growing into a beautiful young lady. I am so proud of her in every respect. My sons are real men. They look directly into the eyes when talking to you. They shake hands with a firm confidence. They stand up for their convictions. They lead like Jesus. They are two true Christian gentlemen, and I am so grateful and proud of the men they have become. Today, both Rob and Greg are preaching the Word of God with boldness and anointed power while serving our Savior with no strings attached. Our daughter-in-law, Annabeth, comes from the finest of Christian homes and is a total joy to be around. We love her so much and are so delighted the Lord gave her to our son.

And so, the part about bearing children and replenishing the earth has real meaning for me. Children are never an accident or an afterthought. This is God's intention. But there is a second reason for marriage.

Reason #2: To provide companionship

Genesis 2:18 establishes, *"It is not good for the man to be alone."* Any questions? My wife, Karyn, is my number-one companion and best friend. We hang around together, laugh together, travel together, plan together, weep together, and sometimes struggle together. This word *companion* literally means "comrade" or "associate." God intended for marriage to have two people, a man and a woman, and for them to become the best of friends, comrades. That is why you leave, cleave, and become one flesh in body, soul, and mind. Two people work together as one unit.

I often tell people, tongue in cheek, that I would rather be with Karyn than anyone else at any given time. The truth is I really mean it. I am blessed to have many wonderful friends. As I have already explained, my sons, my daughter-in-law, and my daughter are not only my children, but also my best friends. I serve the Lord together with the most incredible group of men and women. We call ourselves the Knights of the Round Table and really mean it. We have the best time serving the Lord together, and we have the best time loving one another as true friends. I have Lee and Bill and Harry and Keith and Tom and Rick and John and Jim and Ricky and Dave and the list goes on. But none like Karyn. She is my wife, my lover, my soulmate, and my friend.

Many marriages come into real problems when the children leave home. Have you noticed that? Divorce often occurs after the children are grown. Mom and dad spend all their time, money, and energy on their children as they grow and develop. Then, twenty years later, the children have moved out, mom and dad are finally alone together and . . . nothing. The two people who were once in love find themselves feeling alone. They sit across from each other at the dinner table and wonder, "Who are you?" Their companionship has suffered because they did not invest in it; they did not nourish it.

Am I implying your children are not important? No, certainly not! But I am trying to impress upon your hearts an important principle: according to God's plan, the single most important person to you is your spouse, not your children. If your children are coming before your relationship with your mate, you are in trouble. If not now, you will be in trouble later.

I am in no way implying you focus on your spouse and neglect your children. My children are absolutely one of the greatest joys of my life. But God is the God of order. If you and your wife stop loving each other, you can still give your children every material gift imaginable, yet you have given them nothing. The greatest joy, the greatest blessing you can bestow on your children is that mom and dad love each other. Their hearts will be thrilled as the two of you stick like glue. Though they may moan and say, "Yuck, you two. Stop kissing, that's gross!", deep down (maybe way deep down) they want their mom and dad to be in love, to be best friends more than anything else in the world.

I have a love/hate response to the story of man's creation. I love the part that deals with God's creation of Adam. It really is a great story. God created man in His own image, according to Genesis 1. Here Adam was with everything at his disposal. Think about this for a minute. The Garden of Eden was one unbelievable place. I live in a beautiful place called the Upstate of South Carolina. On one occasion, I was privileged to go and visit my dear friend and mentor, Dr. Billy Graham, in his home in Montreat, North Carolina. The international golfer, statesman, and unsurpassed gentleman, Gary Player; another close friend, Jim Anthony; and I jumped in a helicopter and flew over the mountains to visit the Grahams' together. I wish you could see my pictures of the countryside from a helicopter. Just magnificent! Looks every bit like England at its best. Green and lush, with rolling hills and cascading waterfalls. But nothing like the Garden of Eden, I am sure! Added to this, God had placed alongside Adam every beast of the field and every fowl of the air. He had it all! And yet he was lonely. Not even the very best of the best in terms of nature or even the companionship of animals could satisfy his deepest longing. And so, the Lord God created woman and brought her to him. When Adam laid eyes on her, he probably yelled out, "Aha, at last! Wow!" "Wow!" Roughly translated, "God, you did it!"

So, here we have two reasons for marriage: One is to replenish the earth with children. The other is for companionship. But there is a third reason some find hard to understand.

Reason #3: To prevent sexual sin

I recently preached an entire message on the subject of sexual sin based on 1 Corinthians 5. (If you are serious about your marriage, this sermon would be a helpful tool to order from *The Encouraging Word.*) As Christians striving to follow God's Word in a world that says everything is permissible, we must take advantage of safeguards offered to us. By reading books, listening to our pastors and confidants, as well as being vigilant, we can help prevent sexual sin from seeping into our homes. You see, friends, we have to be proactive here. We have to dispel the notion that says, "This sin could never happen to me." Yes, brother, it could happen to you. Yes, sister, it could happen to you too. This sin has the potential to affect any of us, at almost any time and at almost any place. Satan is constantly looking for a foothold in our lives, a way to destroy us from the inside out. Infidelity is a surefire way to annihilate a family unit and to devastate all those involved. The Bible says God ordained marriage in order to prevent us from behaving immorally. What would happen if I was unfaithful in my marriage and I lost my family? Can I tell you what would happen? I would not be able to continue in this ministry. I would not be able to encourage others regarding their marriages and their families. I would have nothing to say because my talk would be vastly incongruent with my walk. I wouldn't have a leg to stand on because my credibility would be ruined. You know, you can make millions of dollars and climb the corporate ladder to the very top, but if you lose your family, you lose everything.

Let's take a closer look at 1 Corinthians 7:2 (NASB), *"But because of immoralities, each man is to have his own wife, and each woman is to have her own husband."* Did you catch that? God knew that we were vulnerable in this area. He was aware that we would be tempted into sin. So He instituted marriage. He provided a way for us *not* to sin.

The human need for sexual gratification is real. God made every person down to the finest detail, including our sexuality. Sexual curiosity begins at an early age. The onset of puberty is accompanied by a driving impulse to feel, know, and explore every aspect of human sexuality. Restraint and control are taught at every level even as the war rages on in the human body. We are intensely sexual creations, and that drive is a gift from God; yet that drive comes with a great responsibility.

I think we all can agree that immorality is rampant in America today. Let us simply consider the names of some popular shows on television: *Desperate Housewives, Sex in the City, The Bachelor,* and *Wife Swap.* There is a hunger and thirst for unrighteousness. The irony is that *Wife Swap* does not, in any way, explore sexuality. So the question is why have a show on television that carries a sexually suggestive title but has little or nothing to do with sex? Because sex sells! Put the sex in there, and people will all want to watch it. But our society, the television shows we watch, the music we listen to, and basically mainstream America say it's okay, that having an extramarital affair is normal.

Well, it's time for us to be reminded that it is not. It is not moral or okay or anything of the sort. It's wrong, it's immoral, and it devastates lives. Please hear me on this: If you are contemplating this sin, are currently ensnared by this sin, or have been affected by this sin in the past, please think carefully about the things we are talking about here. The enticing, sexy depiction of adultery that society creates is a mirage, an illusion. Internet pornography is now rampant. My dear friend, Anne Graham Lotz, daughter of Billy and Ruth Graham, said in our church recently that she is encountering this terror in almost every congregation across America. Our sons and daughters no longer have to go and look for sexual perversion. They simply have to click on it and it's there!

God blessed us with marriage so we can have a way out. He knows our weak spots and has given us the means to protect ourselves from affairs, one-night stands, prostitution, pornography, and other sexual sins.

Let's continue to read the text in 1 Corinthians 7:2–5 (NASB). Paul wrote these words many years ago, but they are completely relevant to us today.

> *But because of immoralities, each man is to have his own wife, and each woman is to have her own husband. The husband must fulfill his duty to his wife, and likewise also the wife to her husband. The wife does not have authority over her own body, but the husband does; and likewise also the husband does not have authority over his own body, but the wife does. Stop depriving one another, except by agreement for a time, so that you may devote yourselves to prayer, and come together again so that Satan will not tempt you because of your lack of self-control.*

One of the main reasons God has provided the institution of marriage is to prevent sexual sin. This is not always the easiest concept for some people to grasp. And, I might add, especially women. Too many women are abused sexually by inconsiderate and selfish men. And so this directive, understandably, causes such women to think the idea here is that they are sex objects. I have heard war stories of wives who claim they were virtually raped by their over-sexed husbands, some even on their honeymoons. Many men just don't get it. Some have had poor role models. Some have never been taught control and discipline. Some are just plain selfish and arrogant. Some are true chauvinists in their whole approach and attitude toward the fairer sex. Some are just ignorant. The problem is they take these attitudes and faults into the marriage bed with them. And the consequences can be devastating. If we are to fully grasp and understand what Paul is saying here concerning the role each partner plays in marriage, we need to address what I call the golden key and golden rule to marriage.

A. The Golden Key to Marriage

I wish you could see the faces of young couples I have had the privilege of counseling prior to their marriages. And it may be worthwhile to note that I will not agree to marry a couple unless they agree to at least three sessions of premarital counseling with me or with someone I have confidence in recommending to them. This is a long story, but I always begin by talking, in far greater detail than I will in this book, about the golden key to marriage. Most couples, understandably, give all kinds of good, relevant answers to this question, but I have never had a couple give the right answer. The golden key to marriage is that the man is a male and the woman is a female! Yep, I came up with that idea all by myself. What a genius I am. Think about how profound this really is. It's the fundamental issue in marriage, and it is the fundamental reason why so many marriages go south. But this is the way God created us. We are unique and distinct in every way. *Vive la différence!*

I turn to the (blushing) bride-to-be and ask her if she would like her man to be anything less than 100 percent man. The answer is always no. Well, I say, "Then let me share with you what comes with the 100 percent man you are about to marry." And so we begin with an anatomy class that everybody knows about but nobody wants to talk about! Male sexuality is different from female sexuality. We both want to get to the same point, but we sure take a different road getting there. Male needs of gratification are entirely different from the female in almost every expression of sexuality. The almighty male can be completely satisfied sexually in a matter of moments, and he certainly does not need a warm-up period. Nor does his sexuality depend on whether the pictures on the wall are straight, or whether the children are asleep, or if the dishes have been washed, or even if he is tired or not. Need to hear any more? And so it is with the woman. Same result, different approach.

Here is the bottom line. In my opinion, the golden key to marriage is the most neglected area of marriage. Many husbands do not love their wives as females, and many wives do not love their husbands as males. One of the most critical essentials in a marriage has to do with this issue. The number-one assignment for the male is to make it his business to engender, foster, nourish, and celebrate the spirit of femininity that is his wife's heart and soul. This is how God created her. And so it follows that every time the husband demeans his wife in body, he chips away at her soul and spirit. Chipping away comes in small doses and in large chunks. A wandering eye, an unkind word, and an out-and-out affair all have devastating effects on her. Many marriages stay intact because of strong Christian commitment and a total disdain for divorce, but they have very little to show behind the bedroom door. Many marriages die early on while others suffer a slow and painful death.

B. The Golden Rule for Marriage

The question about the golden key is how to put it into practice. What governs this vital notion? It is the golden rule for marriage. Here it is. He comes first. She comes first. Show me a marriage in which the husband and wife try to "out-first" each other, and I will show you a marriage "made in heaven." Simply put, the husband ought to always put his wife first in everything, including the matter of sex. And it has to begin with him because he is the head of the home and he is the man. In practice, this means the male must submit and even deny his own sexual needs in favor of her needs as a female. Besides, it is worth the time and effort, and the rewards are great!

Let me illustrate. Here's a couple who both get up in the morning, ready to go to work. They have chosen a more traditional lifestyle: He has an office job while she stays at home with their small children for the first few years. He eats breakfast hurriedly and storms out the door to make his first appointment. Throughout the day, he is surrounded by other women, some of whom do not operate according to godly principles of sexual behavior. He is very busy making decisions and climbing the corporate ladder of success.

In the meantime, his wife is at home with the little ones all day: cleaning, changing, burping, feeding, and having one serious conversation after another with the washing machine. He arrives home. Regardless of how she thinks she looks or feels, he thinks she looks and feels very inviting. Very sexy. His reaction is immediate. Off to bed! In fact, forget the bed. The kitchen floor will do! He loves her. She's his wife. He's a Christian man. He has principles. Is there anything so far that he has done wrong? Is he a criminal or, even worse, an animal because he wants to be intimate with his wife? Of course not. He's made that way. He's male, a man. All man.

Now, what about her? She wants to rest first. Put her feet up for a while. She really would like to take a long, hot bath with bubbles. The meal needs to be savored, not gobbled up. The family needs to sit down, at the table no less. The television needs to be switched off. Then, the dishes need to be washed, dried, and put away in their proper place. Then, nice music needs to be playing while Dad puts the children to sleep after reading them what seems like an endless version of *The Little Froggie and the Cuddly Brown Bear*. Then, late at night, after romance has filled the air with its fragrance, well . . . just maybe! Now, is there anything she has done so far wrong? Of course not! She's made that way. She's female, a woman. All woman.

What's the solution? He comes first; she comes first. This is how it works. The more he puts her first, the more she will put him first. It's the law of God.

Faithfulness in marriage is not an option, and it's never too late to start all over again. It will be like the dawning of a new day.

However, sexual sins are rampant in our world today, even within the confines of marriage. Many men and women have the idea that the grass is greener on the other side or that the chase will be just as exciting as it was when they were teenagers. Television shows and movies portray marital infidelity as something thrilling and fulfilling. But if you have ever experienced the damage that sexual sins bring, you know the consequences are great. Let's talk briefly about the consequences of unfaithfulness in marriage.

The Judgment of God. I wish I could get around this, but the judgment of God is the number-one consequence of unfaithfulness in marriage. We do not like to think about God's judgment, but the Bible is very clear on this topic. Galatians 5:19 and 5:21 say that those who are sexually immoral will not inherit the kingdom of God. Please do not close your heart to God's Word. I have good news for you if you will continue with me, but if you close your heart right now, I can't help.

Let me tell you what happens to a man or woman who is morally unfaithful. The first thing he or she will do is run away. Sin always runs and hides from the truth. Darkness has no part with the Light. First Corinthians 6:18 says, *"Flee from sexual immorality."* Ephesians 5:6 (NASB) says, *"Let no one deceive you with empty words, for because of these things* [immorality and unfaithfulness in marriage] *the wrath of God comes upon the sons of disobedience."* Do not run away and hide from the truth, but instead run away from immorality. Run to God and to the truth of His Word. God is willing to forgive those who are unfaithful in marriage if they will only turn to Him. Other negative consequences may not be avoided, but your willingness to repent and turn from your sin is imperative in order to avoid the judgment of God. So, what are the consequences of unfaithfulness? Number one is the judgment of God.

The Devastation of the Family. Marital unfaithfulness not only impacts the adult individuals involved, but young family members as well. When you violate your marriage, you devastate your children. A person caught up in adultery may rationalize and say, "I love my children, but I simply do not love my spouse." Nevertheless, the children are devastated. A child often feels betrayed when a parent seems willing to choose another person over their love for their children. The children's feelings also become evident to the parent. Sooner or later, the parents' hearts will begin to harden in order to deal with the pain they know they've caused their children. They may develop bitterness and anger in their hearts that will be lived out in their relationships. Often, these behaviors are passed down for generations. Children will see the resentment and begin to emulate it. No matter how much you think you can control the situation, you can't. Your children will pay the price for your marital infidelity.

I'm certain that if you choose to be unfaithful (and it is a choice), your children will be devastated. They will be pulled between parents; they will feel confused; they will feel abandoned. If the marriage disintegrates and the children live with one parent, they, in their minds, are betraying the other. Children often live with one parent during the week and the other parent on the weekends. We have children and youth in our church whose attendance records show absences every other week because they are house-hopping. It will be a sad day in your life when you wake up and find that you have made a terrible mistake that cannot be reversed. The greatest thing you can do for your children is to love and live in peace with your spouse.

Marital unfaithfulness not only devastates your children, but ravages the life of your spouse as well. Genesis 2:24 say to us that when a man and woman marry they become one flesh. What can be worse than someone with whom you have become one in body and spirit betraying you sexually or emotionally? If we are one in flesh, it would be like having your arm ripped off or you leg torn away—pure devastation. Many who are affected by this ask, "How am I supposed to function now?" Years may pass before a spouse recovers from the heartbreak of an extramarital affair. Often, healing never comes. The consequences of marital unfaithfulness are grave for your children and your spouse regardless of how you rationalize your behavior.

The Testimony of the Gospel. Not only do you face the judgment of God and your family is utterly devastated, but your testimony of the gospel is darkened as well. God is talking to believers in this passage. I can understand when an unbeliever sins, but when it comes to a believer who says that he or she loves Jesus Christ, there is no excuse. The testimony of the gospel is heard through everyday actions of Christians. You have a covenant before God to live the gospel through your actions. Some people have suggested that Christians are the only Bible that some people will read.

Throughout the Bible, darkness represents sin. When believers have unconfessed sin in their lives, darkness covers the gospel. Others will not be able to see Jesus Christ through your life when the sin of marital unfaithfulness veils it. Repenting of sin and living a life of obedience to God dispels the darkness, and the light of Jesus Christ is evident for all to see. Please hear me here. If you have been party to this sort of sin, you can be forgiven. This is not the unpardonable sin. God wants you back, desperately. But you must confess. You must come clean to God, to yourself, and to those you hurt. Your testimony as a Christian will be darkened by sin if you let it fester and grow. This is true with any sin; whether it's lying, cheating, or stealing, sin shrouds your face from God. Light has no place with the dark.

The Fabric of Society. Marital unfaithfulness burrows into the fabric of society. If you look at the history of all the great empires, you will see a common thread. Consider the Roman Empire, for example. It fell because rampant immorality seized the family structure. They fed off one another; they gave one another an excuse to be immoral. And what was left? A collapsed, corrupt society was all that remained. If we understand the Word of God, the biggest question facing America today is not "Who is going to be in the White House?" but rather "What role do Christian core values play in our society?"

It does not matter what anybody says. It does not matter what Oprah Winfrey, George W. Bush, or Don Wilton has to say about these things. It only matters what God says, and His Word is plain. The consequences of marital unfaithfulness will come sooner or later. Galatians 6:7–8 admonishes, *"Do not be deceived: God cannot be mocked. A man reaps what he sows. The one who sows to please his sinful nature, from that nature will reap destruction; the one who sows to please the Spirit, from the Spirit will reap eternal life."*

The Seven Steps to Healing in Marriage

I have been promising throughout this chapter that relief was coming, that a new day can begin. And here it is. I have configured a seven-step plan to help you recognize sin, turn from it, and find hope again. God has put the following steps to healing in my heart, and I share them with you so you can write them upon your heart. Use these steps to heal your marriage whether you are still married, divorced, guilty of unfaithfulness, or whether you have simply done things that you know are not pleasing in God's sight.

When a marriage begins to fail, people often run and hide. Sometimes they look around for someone to help. If you are caught up in unfaithfulness in your marriage, what can you do about it? If you are contemplating an affair, where can you turn? These steps may prevent the serious consequences that sooner or later arise due to unfaithfulness in marriage.

Step #1—Stop It Immediately.

Whatever you are doing that is immoral and in violation of the sanctity of your marriage, stop it immediately. Do not say, "Well, I need to think about this." There is nothing to take into consideration. There is no excuse as far as God is concerned. Do not rationalize your behavior. You may say, "We have never actually *had* sex." Well, an affair of the heart is simply a precursor to a sexual affair. Stop it immediately before it is too late! Do not try and wean yourself away. Stop. Turn. Run.

Step #2—Confess to God Truthfully.

First John 1:9 says, *"If we confess our sins, he is faithful and just and will forgive us our sins and purify us from all unrighteousness."* Confess it to God truthfully. Be honest and straightforward with your prayer. "Lord, I have sinned in Your sight. I have been unfaithful in my marriage." Confess to God truthfully. God's forgiveness will cover us. If we confess, He will forgive.

Step #3—Repent to Your Family Humbly.

The offended party is your family. Go to them and repent to them one on one, eyeball to eyeball. Do it with the utmost humility. Do not rationalize your behavior. Do not go with strings attached. "I'm coming to tell you that I have done this wrong, but I want you to know that you need to do this for me." This doesn't work! God doesn't accept that; God doesn't operate with strings attached. Apologize, confess, and recognize that this will not be an easy thing for them to hear. Be patient with your family as they digest the fact that they have been betrayed.

Step #4—Go Back Home Instantly.

The longer you stay away from your home, the less likely it is that you will ever bring your home back together—golden rule. I hear people say to me all the time, "Well, we're just in a trial separation," Excuse me? There is no trial separation as far as God is concerned. Go back home instantly! If you have moved out or you have been deservedly kicked out, put things in line and go back home, even if you have to sleep in the doghouse. You must go back home. You cannot do it on the telephone. You've got to be with the ones you have offended, as hard as it is.

Step #5—Accept God's Forgiveness Completely.

I love this! Here is what happens. When I confess to God, confess to my spouse, go back home, stop what I am doing, and do what God's telling me to, *then* I am able to accept God's forgiveness completely. Now why completely? Because He takes my sin and casts it as far as the East is from the West; He remembers it no more. I am going to be quite honest with you—we struggle with that. I want to make an important announcement: if you have done these things, God has forgiven you, not partly, but completely. Boom, just like that! Take peace from that truth. If we have honestly and humbly asked for forgiveness, God is pleased. Period—end of discussion.

Step #6—Understand Consequences Realistically.

Sin has consequences. This sin in particular has many consequences: pregnancy, abortion, divorce, violence, kidnapping, and revenge just to name a few. Know that when you come clean with your spouse, he or she will not jump at the chance to throw his or her arms around you and forgive you on the spot. People don't work like God. Life cannot be "business as usual." It will be very hard, very uncomfortable, and very challenging. You are not going to occupy positions of spiritual leadership at first, and you should not. You may not even be able to occupy positions of leadership in society. When trust is broken, it takes time to rebuild. This naturally brings us to the next step.

Step #7—Rebuild Your Life Intentionally.

When you rebuild your life intentionally, you are understanding consequences realistically. When something is broken down, you must rebuild it in order for it to be functional again. It takes time, patience, and love, but God will do it. Maybe you are asking in your heart, "Pastor, since I have sinned, can God ever use me again?" Yes, He can! Let me tell you about some people God used despite their less than perfect record: Consider Noah—he was a drunk. Abraham was too old. Isaac was a daydreamer. Jacob was a liar. Leah was ugly. (I'm sorry to say that!) Moses had a stuttering problem. Gideon was afraid. Sampson was a womanizer. Rahab was a prostitute. Jeremiah and Timothy were too young. David had an affair with a woman outside of his marriage and was a murderer. Elijah was suicidal. Isaiah preached naked (I'm not going there, let's move on). Jonah ran from God. John the Baptist ate bugs. (Well, no sin there, but that's just weird). Peter denied Christ. The disciples fell asleep while praying. Martha worried about everything. The Samaritan woman was divorced multiple times. Paul, formerly Saul, was a religious persecutor. And, here it is—Lazarus was dead. (Not a sin, I know, but pretty impressive, huh?) God used them all. And God will use you in spite of your sin, too.

Now watch this: You have sinned. You have messed up. But, thankfully, that doesn't matter to God. If we are reconciled, squared away with God, then He can still use us. The greatest people in the Bible are those with the poorest track records. Now, you may be thinking, "Wait a minute, Dr. Wilton, what I'm hearing you say is that my life is not over?" No, it is not over, my friend. "You think God can ever use me again?" Yes! I absolutely do. Some of the people I have seen used the most in their families, in society, and in the Lord's work have been people who have messed up big time. But they took definitive steps, and God healed their lives.

If you are serious about living your life for the Lord, be faithful in marriage. Don't let a moment of pleasure stop you from accomplishing His purpose for your life. Though we may stumble and fall, even sprain an ankle along the way, we've got to get up and keep on running the race. Don't let sin cause you to quit running. Don't give up because you have fallen down. After all, that's exactly what Satan wants you to do. If he can get you to move farther away from God, his job is done. Don't let Satan win. Recognize your sin, repent to those you've hurt, and run!

One of the greatest joys in the world is to hear what people say about loved ones who have passed into the presence of the Lord Jesus. My own parents, John and Rhodabelle Wilton, and my wife's parents, Ed and Mirth Bolton, have spent a lifetime serving our Savior and Lord. Our joy has been a lifetime of memories that range from vacations to birthday celebrations, from meals to movies, and great moments of love and laughter together. But when that day comes when God calls one and all of them home to be with Him in heaven, it will be said, "I'll see you at the finish line." The greatest of all gifts under the Lordship of Jesus Christ in their lives is the fact that our parents loved one another and remained faithful to one another all the way to the finish line. What an unspeakable gift!

THE SEVENTH CHAPTER

The Unattainable Illusion

Not that I speak from want, for I have learned to be content in whatever circumstances I am. I know how to get along with humble means, and I also know how to live in prosperity; in any and every circumstance I have learned the secret of being filled and going hungry, both of having abundance and suffering need.

—Philippians 4:11–12 (NASB)

Scripture Reference: Hebrews 13:5–6
Keep your lives free from the love of money and be content with what you have, because God has said, "Never will I leave you; never will I forsake you." So we say with confidence, "The Lord is my helper; I will not be afraid. What can man do to me?"

I magine with me, if you will, we are walking along together in a desert. The temperature is hot and the air is dry. The sand is dusty; it's sticking to our perspiring legs and feet. We've been traveling this path for several miles, and we are getting thirsty. The bottles of water we packed are already gone. If we only had a sip or two more, we could make it to our destination. As we descend down a small hill, we see a lake. It is glistening in the sun. It is beautiful. Typically, we wouldn't dream of drinking out of a lake, but today the water looks glorious. Our pace quickens as we get closer and closer to the cool, clear water that awaits us. But when we reach what seemed to be our saving grace, we find it isn't there. What we thought was a lake containing precious, thirst-quenching water is actually a mirage, an unattainable illusion.

I think our society conveys this picture in every aspect of life. It's always telling us to upgrade this, expand that, and improve the other. We are in a consumer-driven culture that demands we strive to *have* the best and to *be* the best. This may come in the form of a home, a car, a job, our children, or our overall status in life. Regardless, we are on a continual, constant search for that ever-elusive lake in the desert. Just around the next corner will be our big break. We'll finally hit it big! Maybe that thirst-quenching water in the lonely, dry desert looks like finally being out of debt, having that child we've been hoping for, getting that big promotion, attaining our master's degree, or finding the love of our life. We are conditioned to believe that if we buy the right stuff, wear the right clothes, and hang out with the right people, we will be happy and content. But we quickly find that we have to buy bigger stuff, more expensive clothes, and meet more interesting people to maintain that same level of happiness. Searching for contentment through material gain or achievement will yield only vain attempts on our part. It's like we're on a bike, pedaling as fast as we can, but going nowhere. We are sitting, still spinning our wheels.

Throughout the course of this chapter, we will gain a sense of where contentment comes from, how we can attain it, and what it takes to hold on to it. But before we get started, let's take a second to answer the following questions carefully and candidly in order to determine where we stand on this issue:

1. Do you wish your life were different?
2. Does the grass appear greener on the other side?
3. Are you happy with yourself?
4. Do you like your life?
5. Are you satisfied with what you have?

I would say most of us struggle daily with the concept of being content. There are books, CDs, and Web sites devoted to making more money, finding the love of our life, and climbing the ladder of success.

Contentment is not a popular word in our ever-changing, goal-oriented society. As a matter of fact, contentment is often viewed as complacency or indolence. If you aren't striving to land that big account, to make partner, or to buy the house of your dreams, you must be lazy. Somehow it came to be that unless we are looking ahead to the next big thing we must not care. I have a good friend who is really into electronic gadgets: razor-thin cell phones, megapixel digital cameras, MP3 players, iPods, and portable DVD players with the latest upgrades. Just take his last purchase, for example. He recently bought a very small and very sleek cell phone. It has every function you could possibly imagine. It's the latest, hottest thing on the market. But do you know what happened not even two months later? They came out with a newer, more advanced model. Now what? The phone he bought a blink ago is now "the older model." And so the chase ensues once again.

Now, I don't blame this issue on society entirely. I think the chase has been going on since the beginning of time. Literally since Adam and Eve, man has been searching for more. We are peculiar in this way. For some mysterious reason we think, "The grass will definitely be greener on the other side. I just need to take a quick peek and see what I'm missing." In my understanding, contentment is an attitude, a lifestyle. As Socrates, the great Greek philosopher, put it, "He who is not contented with what he has would not be contented with what he would like to have." Having more, having the latest, or having the best does not guarantee happiness or contentment. It has to come from the inside out. Until we learn to be content within ourselves, we'll just keep looking for more. Happiness will only be a mirage—a place you long to go but a place you will never quite reach.

In Hebrews 13:5–6, the author is saying that we are to be content with ourselves, our lives, and everything therein. This is *not* to say that we shouldn't want what's best for our families, friends, and selves. It is to say, however, that our focus, our drive in life comes from our satisfaction being found in the Lord. Beyond that we should have nothing left to want. If we have all the possessions in the world but lack love *for* and faith *in* the Lord Jesus Christ, we have nothing. Now, I know what most of you are thinking at this point: "I'm a Christian but somehow I still seem to struggle with being content in every circumstance. How do I stop chasing the big illusive dream? How do I stop grasping for that unattainable illusion?" I'm going to suggest some basic guidelines. I call them my "Golden Rules of Contentment." These will assist us as we deal with this real-life struggle. As we head toward the finish line, it is imperative we not only understand the true meaning of contentment but we also learn how to run the race of life in a fashion that exemplifies true Christ-like contentedness. So, lace up your sneakers because here we go!

Three Golden Rules of Contentment

As we begin this section, I want to take a second and underline something very important: Being content in every situation means we do not let our circumstances dictate our responses and our behaviors. That is, we remain consistent in our spirits no matter what's going on in the world around us. Now, I don't have to tell you how difficult that can be. Life is filled with inconsistencies, challenges, struggles, and areas colored in gray. Often, it feels like things around us are spinning out of control. We've gotta go here, we've gotta do this, and we've gotta say that! Contentment is fleeting because we are so distracted by the ever-changing world in which we live. How can we possibly expect to find satisfaction in a place where technology, emotions, and circumstances change so rapidly?

Everywhere we look today, it seems we are being challenged at the point of our contentment. Take, for example, someone like LeBron James, who plays for the Cleveland Cavaliers and will probably be the next Michael Jordan. This remarkable young man signed contracts through Nike and others to make hundreds of millions of dollars while he was still a teenager, just eighteen years old. As a result, many athletes in America look at him and say, "I want a better deal. I want a better endorsement." They spend their lives never satisfied with what they have or where they are. And though most of us aren't looking at million-dollar deals, we do the exact same thing in our own lives. We need a "cooler" car because our friend just got a great-looking ride and now ours doesn't look so shiny anymore. Or our neighbor just put in a pool and now our home seems boring and plain.

I truly believe the day and age in which we live fosters a spirit of discontentment, especially among our teens. Relatively speaking, many of them have everything life has to offer. While this is certainly not the case with many who are less fortunate, millions of teenagers grow up surrounded by the trappings of plenty. Anyone who has ever been to Spartanburg, South Carolina, will know about the Beacon. This restaurant was started by an incredible man, John White, who is not only a friend to me but also to thousands of others. He epitomizes giving. He has meant so much to his community in so many different ways. He is also a member of my church. While the Beacon has been host to almost every political candidate running for almost every kind of office in the United States of America, it has become known for the wonderful, fattening, and excessive loads of food it delivers. A person who orders a chili cheese-a-plenty gets exactly that . . . a-plenty! It is loaded down in a major way. In all the years I have observed others eating at the Beacon, I seriously doubt anyone has ever finished what they have on their plates. Now, while it is tremendous fun to go to the Beacon, it is a commentary on ourselves. We always want more than we can handle. Our "eyes are too big for our stomachs." We are never satisfied. Moms struggle to "just be Moms," Dads struggle to "just be Dads," teens struggle to "just enjoy being teens," and there is a great restlessness about. You can feel it everywhere. Writing his letter to the church at Philippi, Paul spoke of the learning process, which is essential to being content, no matter where we find ourselves. We can acquire this habit. And when we do, we are set free from anxiety.

Well, I'm about to show you something that is remarkable. These three golden rules will greatly assist the serious Christian in bringing about true contentment. As fundamental principles, they will exemplify how we can find satisfaction and contentment in an ever-changing world. These principles will show us how to stand still and be consistent during times of chaos, comparison, and contradiction.

GOLDEN RULE #1:
Never love *what* you have more than what you *do* with what you have.

Look at this. Read it over and over and over again. Write it down in a place where you will see it often. Never love *what* you have more than what you *do* with what you have. For example, I have a very nice car. (And, by the way, I think most Americans have a love affair with their cars. I mean we give them names, for crying out loud!) Nevertheless, here is what God says to me, "Don Wilton, I've given you a car to drive, and now you have a choice. Either love what you have—love your car, that is your idol, that is your baby—or love what I am enabling you to do with what you have." Now, it's not hard to figure out which choice is the better one. Obviously, God desires for us to fix our eyes on serving others rather than finding fulfillment in material possessions. So, let's look at this.

What can I do with my car? I can go and pick up my sons and daughter at school. That is a real blessing! I can go to the grocery store and help my wife out. That is a real blessing! I can use my car to go and visit somebody in the hospital. That is a real blessing! I can take a trip somewhere: I can go on vacation; I can get to the church; I can get to my friends. I'm mobile. I can get from point A to point B with next to no effort on my part. God is saying to me that I need to love what I do with what I have far more than loving what I have. My car, in this case, is only a *means* to an end. It's not the end.

In our Scripture reference, Hebrews 13:5–6, the author uses

money as an illustration because it is a logical, tangible thing everyone can relate to. At one time or another, we all have been ensnared by the love of what we have, i.e., the love of money. Money is not evil. It is the love of money that is evil. Knowing this, we must make a concerted effort to focus on what we can do with what we have instead of focusing solely on what we have. Jesus taught that it is harder for a rich man to enter the kingdom of God than it is for a camel to go through the eye of a needle (see Matthew 19:24; Mark 10:25; Luke 18:25). Now, why do you think He would say something like that? Why do you think the same thing was covered in three different Gospels? I think it's because Jesus knew how vulnerable we are on this issue. He knew that we all have a case of the "grass is always greener" syndrome. That is why He said it hundreds of years ago and why it still holds true today. From Adam and Eve to Abraham, to the great King David, to the twelve devoted disciples, and to you and me today, we long for more. We have restless souls. But the Lord Jesus Christ came to satisfy our hunger and to quench our thirst. The contentment we find in objects, money, material possessions, or achievements will never compare to the satisfaction we can find by resting in the hands of our God.

I have a friend of many years. Before I met him, I had heard about him and seen him from a distance. He was a blessed man in so many ways. Just one look at his lifestyle would tell the whole story. He had worked hard and was obviously brilliant at what he did. Making money was his life, he told me later. And he was very good at it. Everything he touched turned to gold. One day he ran headlong into the Lord Jesus Christ and his life's focus changed. Today he makes more money than ever before, but something is totally different about him. There is a joy on his face and a sparkle in his eye. I asked him some time ago what the difference was between now and then. "Oh," he exclaimed quickly, "it's no longer about what I have but what I do with what I have!" I have another very close friend who years ago struggled to make payroll from one week to another. Today he is doing things for others one can only imagine. He is helping children, he is helping adults, and he is engaged in so many wonderful projects of kindness and generosity. He told me recently that wealth in and of itself is meaningless. To borrow a phrase, "it will leave you empty" if all you have is what you have rather than all you do is what you have.

So many people have never learned this great truth. So many hold on like a drowning man holding on to a passing twig. The law of God tells us to give and it will be given back abundantly. You are not going to take it with you anyway. I remember visiting with two elderly people some years ago. They wanted me to hear their final wishes. As I sat there with their attorney, I wanted to cry as I heard of their accumulated wealth. Here were these two, living in a small little home, musty and dark, arguing with one another, and a bank balance that could have given so much joy and meaning not only to themselves but to countless numbers of people, organizations, and, most importantly, to the on-going ministry of the Lord Jesus Christ. But no! Sadly, when they did pass away, their estate became embroiled in bitter dispute. Half their money went to organizations and institutions they could not have had any idea about, let alone what was going to happen to all their money, and Uncle Sam kept the lion's share.

You see, my friend, this principle will govern your past, present, and future. It will release you and set you free. You will run for the finish line well.

GOLDEN RULE #2:
Never crave what you do not have.

I want you to listen to this one—I'm begging you. Do not go through life craving what you do not have. If you do this, you will make yourself miserable. One of my very good friends in college, an old roommate of mine, came from a well-to-do family. His father owned a large corporation, and my friend had very little to worry about in the way of finances. I, on the other hand, juggled three jobs and worked my way through school. This friend of mine had plenty of time to study, time to play sports, and time to hang out with our friends while I scrambled to make ends meet. During the summers, he had a part-time job which he hated and often complained about. And, as you can probably imagine, this never set well with me. There I was, working thirty hours a week, taking summer classes, and trying to pay my bills while he's grumbling about a measly ten hours a week during three months of the year. Give me a break! Well, one day his mother was in town, and I was just about to my breaking point. We were all upstairs and I flippantly muttered something about his surplus of money and my lack thereof. Though I don't remember exactly what I said, I do remember exactly what was said to me. That day, in our little apartment, my friend's mother spoke some of the most profound words I had ever heard. She said, "You know, everyone has their own cross to bear." Wow. I had never thought about it like that before. I was always more concerned with what *he* had than I was with what *I* had. I never realized that he, too, had a cross to bear. My focus was on what I had to bear; it was on the things that he had which I often found myself craving. Those short, simple words his mother spoke helped to change my perspective and realize that the grass isn't always greener on the other side. It, too, has to be mowed.

Discontentment comes in many forms, very often resulting in a restlessness for a number of reasons. Some of us are not happy with what we have, some are not satisfied with where we are in life, some are not pleased with who we are, and some of us aren't fulfilled in who we've become. If you struggle with the "keeping up with the Joneses" syndrome like most Americans, then you are constantly comparing yourself with others. I'm sure you catch yourself thinking, "Look what they've got," "It must be so great to be them," and "I bet they never have to worry about money." The Joneses syndrome is simply a bad case of craving what you do not have. It is the epitome of discontentment. As I learned in college, wanting what someone else has does not guarantee happiness. It actually has quite the opposite effect. Bitterness and jealousy will crop up in your heart. You will look at your own life with a critical eye completely bypassing all the blessings God has given you. Craving what others have will only make you more dissatisfied with your life because your focus will be on what you *don't* have instead of what you *do* have. The next time you decide to measure yourself against someone else, just remember the lesson I learned from a dear friend's mother—everyone has his or her own cross to bear. Just because you don't see the struggles doesn't mean they don't have them. You will drive yourself crazy if your focus is on what someone else has because there will always be someone bigger, faster, stronger, richer, smarter, and more beautiful than you are. Our job is to focus on and be thankful for all the gifts and blessings God has given us—period!

Golden Rule #3:
Never covet what others have.

Consider this carefully: never covet what others have. Now, you might be asking, "Pastor, what's the difference between coveting and craving? Didn't we just cover this?" Good question, but craving is a strong desire for something usually temporary in nature. For example, a lot of times this word is used in regards to food. "Oh, I'm craving something sweet. Maybe a chocolate doughnut would do the trick, or some rocky road ice cream would hit the spot." If we are watching our waistlines, like most of us are these days, we opt for a healthy snack instead. But you know as well as I do that this kind of craving will not subside until we pop a few M & Ms or take a bite of that forbidden cake. A craving is a pull, a draw, and oftentimes we won't be satisfied until we get it. But more times than not, a craving is temporary in that it provides only passing satisfaction. You see, friends, when we crave something someone else has, we want it for ourselves and sometimes we will go broke (or gain weight) until we get it. Craving certainly creates discontentment in our lives, and it causes us to overlook our blessings. Coveting is a bit more in depth. It, too, creates discontentment in our lives, but it also overtakes our lives. Coveting is being greedy, having a compulsion to hoard all we can get. Coveting, by definition, refers to the grasping of wealth with the intention to hoard it. It is very selfish and ambitious with little to no regard for anyone else.

One of the hardest things for people to do is to be blessed of the Lord. I realize this sounds strange, but we need to pray for people who have really been blessed. Can I tell you why? The more people are blessed materially, the more others will criticize them. Some people spend half their lives criticizing wealthy people, people of means, people who are blessed materially. They criticize what they drive, their wonderful family, or their beautiful home. Be careful not to walk around with a big chip on your shoulder, being frustrated with God or yourself about what others have that you do not. You see, when you crave what you do not have and you covet what others have, you are doing two things. First, you are breaking one of God's commandments: "Thou shalt not covet." Second, you are buying into the root of all evil. You are listening to Satan as he whispers in your ear, "You need that. Wouldn't your life be better if you had what they had? Go out there and do whatever it takes to get it. You can make it happen." God sees this and says, "Stop it. Be content with what I have given you. Quit chasing after something I have not chosen to give you." His Word covers this clearly in Luke 12:15, *"Be on your guard against all kinds of greed; a man's life does not consist in the abundance of his possessions."* Coveting your neighbors' material wealth will only lead to a dead end. Obsessing and chasing after someone else's lot in life is pointless and useless. If you want to be content, quit looking around and start looking up!

The Consequences of Discontentment

Did you know that there are consequences that come with being discontent beyond just being discontent? In other words, if you love what you have more than what you do with what you have, if you crave what you do not have, and if you covet what other people have, then you will not only be dissatisfied with yourself, your stuff, and your life but three other consequences might also occur. Let's look at what could happen:

1. Your character will be flawed.

One thing I think we can all agree on: you cannot buy character. It will not be on sale at any mall; you can't pick it up at the grocery store. Character is made. It comes from down deep. It's your integrity, your person, your soul, what you stand for, what surfaces when you are shaken. If you are spending your life discontent with everything that happens, if you are always complaining, if you are never satisfied, then you have a serious character flaw. Let's put this in a personal perspective. Have you ever been around a person who is always griping, complaining, coveting, and craving for more? Never satisfied? Do you like them very much? Be honest, now. Few people wake up in the morning and find themselves thinking, "What a day. I think I'll just go hang around with old discontented what's-his-face!" Every church has them. They are the ones who come to church meetings and believe the Lord has sent them there on a mission. When question time comes around, they are the ones who stand up and say, "Pastor, I'd like to share a word of discontentment with the congregation. God asked me to do this." Ask anyone around and they will tell you his character is flawed.

2. Your motives will be distorted.

Motive has often been defined as the reason you do something. This is an important issue to be tested. Have you ever gone to a restaurant with someone because they're always asking you if you will go out and eat with them? Then you understand the reason they ask is because they want you to pick up the tab. When the check comes, they "outfumble you" or they pretend not to see it. You pick it up, and the person stammers around saying, "Oops, oh, ugh, gah, le, met, let me get that." You reply, "No, I'll pay it." And they quickly say, "Okay, if you insist."

My wife and I made up our minds years ago that we would not allow other people to pay for us. Now, I want you to understand what I mean. Maybe you are thinking, "Pastor, you are magnificent beyond yourself." Well, that's another issue entirely. Seriously though, my philosophy in life is that I do not expect other people to pay for me. I do not out-fumble people. It does not matter how many people are there, what kind of group is there, what they have or do not have. I will pay my way, and I will do everything I can to pay for others who are with me. I do not expect other people to pay for me. Watch yourself with this one. Check your motives to ensure they are pure and pleasing to the Lord. You would be amazed at the number of people I know who make little or no effort to bless others. And you would be amazed at the number of people I know who seem to be on a mission in life to bless others at every turn and on every occasion. It is a small wonder such people are blessed themselves. I truly believe the Lord simply wants to bless us. And one of the ways He determines who He will bless is by watching how we spontaneously bless others with no strings attached. Be the one!

3. Your blessings will be limited.

God knows your heart, and He will not bless a heart full of discontent. You show me a selfish person, someone who is discontent, who loves what they have more than what they do with what they have, who craves what they do not have, who covets what others have, and I will show you a person God chooses not to bless. Though His desire is to bless us beyond measure, He won't if we aren't thankful for those blessings He has already given us. Do not forget what the Lord has done for you. Do not neglect what He has given you. Deuteronomy 6:10–12 says:

When the LORD your God brings you into the land he swore to your fathers, to Abraham, Isaac and Jacob, to give you—a land with large, flourishing cities you did not build, houses filled with all kinds of good things you did not provide, wells you did not dig, and vineyards and olive groves you did not plant—then when you eat and are satisfied, be careful that you do not forget the LORD, who brought you out of Egypt, out of the land of slavery.

Some of you are saying, "I'm glad he's not talking about me. I would never do that to God. I'm thankful for everything." Well, the proof is in the pudding. Let's see where we stand. Ask yourself these following questions:

1. Do I complain about my status in life?
2. Do I want a bigger home or a newer car?
3. Am I willing to share *whatever* I have with others without any conditions or strings attached?
4. Am I content in my heart even when material things aren't as I'd like them to be?
5. Do I long for more?
6. Do I long for something better?

How did you do? Were you honest? Was it eye-opening? You know, it will be sad to stand before God one day and see all the blessings He had in store for us, but because of our discontent, those blessings were limited; we missed out.

Being content is a condition of the heart. Contentment will not come from having more or having better. It is the state of our heart regardless of our external situation or surroundings. If your heart is not content, then your perspective will always be shrouded, foggy. *"Whoever loves money never has money enough; whoever loves wealth is never satisfied with his income. This too is meaningless. As goods increase, so do those who consume them. And what benefit are they to the owner except to feast his eyes on them?"* (Ecclesiastes 5:10–11).

The only way to find true contentment is to realize first that this is your life as it is right now. Changes may come, but for now "this" is where you are. Second, appreciate what you have already been given. Look up from your book right now and glance around you. What do you see that you can thank God for? Third, understand that as a sinner, you are not entitled to a-n-y-t-h-i-n-g! It is God who blesses even though we do not deserve a thing. Remember that.

Be content where you are. Learn to grow where you are planted. To borrow a golfing phrase, "play the ball where it lies." Thank God for what you have but, most importantly, love what you can do with what you have. Do not crave or covet those things you see around you. Don't let a discontented spirit be your trademark. Remember the words of the wise King Solomon, the man who had everything money could buy but led a life searching for more, *Whoever loves money never has money enough* (Ephesians 5:10). Keep your life free from the love of things and full of a love for God. Only Jesus can quench your thirst and feed your cravings. Contentment will be yours if your focus is on God instead of that elusive illusion in the desert. And you will finish well!

THE EIGHTH CHAPTER

Follow the Leader

---

*"Let us carefully observe those good qualities wherein our enemies excel us;
and endeavor to excel them, by avoiding what is faulty,
and imitating what is excellent in them."*

—Plutarch

Scripture Reference: Hebrews 13:7–8
*Remember your leaders, who spoke the word of God to you.
Consider the outcome of their way of life and imitate their faith.
Jesus Christ is the same yesterday and today and forever.*

Today, we're going to play a game. Here are the rules:

1. Select a leader or a "head of the line."
2. Line up behind said leader.
3. Mimic the actions of the leader.

Game Objective: To become the new line leader.

So, are you ready to play?

We have all heard of the popular children's game Follow the Leader, right? It's a game of imitation. It's about following the head of the line. Although this parallel might seem a bit too childlike for your taste, this is exactly what Hebrews 13:7 is telling us to do: imitate the faith of spiritual leaders. In this instance, let's start with defining who spiritual leaders are.

In Hebrews, we see Jesus Christ used as a prime example—a perfect example, I should say. As Christians, we know we ought to follow in the footsteps of Christ. This is pretty much a no-brainer. Follow Christ. Well, besides our Lord, there are other wonderful depictions of faith in the Bible. The pages are filled with spiritual leaders who are noteworthy and exceptional. Obviously, Christ is our paramount example, and none other can come close to leading a life so perfect and pure as did the Lord Jesus Christ. However, in His Word, He provides us with human patterns we can emulate. Now, don't misunderstand me. These verses are not telling us to be copycats of other people. He is not telling us to be duplicates or to be followers of men. He is simply telling us to consider their way of life and imitate their faith.

Throughout the Bible, there is a host of people just like you and me who are riddled with faults. "How in the world can we learn from them?" you might ask. "Why wouldn't we just want to keep our eyes focused on Jesus and only listen to what He teaches?" I say, go for it. Follow Jesus; imitate Him. But please don't dismiss the vast reservoir of knowledge and wisdom which comes from many of the spiritual leaders mentioned in the Bible. In some cases, these guys were actually there. They saw the miracles; they witnessed the healings; they watched the bush burn; they saw the waters part. Their perspectives are treasured and precious aspects of Jesus' life in the New Testament and of God's work in the Old. We have many wonderful giants of the faith to imitate: Moses, Abraham, Paul, Job, and the list goes on and on. But what exactly does that mean? How do we imitate the *faith* of another person? Number one: we observe their conduct. Number two: we put what we've learned into practice.

#1—Observe Their Conduct

We learn to imitate others by observing their conduct. If you plan to imitate other people, you must watch them first, study their mannerisms, notice their behaviors, and listen intently to their language. Remember our game? In order to follow the leader, we must watch closely and notice the leader's subtle and overt actions.

Children are unbelievable imitators. It really is quite precious to watch them in action. They hover around us and seem to cling to every word we say and every action we do. Parents, watch what you say and do around those sweet ears because your words and actions *will* be mimicked in one way or another. It certainly catches us off guard when a child decides he is going to mimic something a parent has said. And you know most of the time, it's not at the right place, it's not at the right time, and it's certainly not the right thing to say. Sometimes it's cute and ends up being funny, like my friend's three-year-old son, for instance. The little boy, his father, and grandfather were driving along in the car one day, and the little boy was chattering away in the back seat. The next thing they know the little boy loudly spouts out, "A man's gotta do what a man's gotta do." Of course, the father and grandfather thought this was the funniest thing they had ever heard and immediately cracked up laughing. And this from a three-year-old! Fortunately, this was a saying he picked up from watching *Veggie Tales*, a Christian cartoon, over and over again.

Unfortunately, though, the stories of emulations don't always turn out so funny. There are plenty of things our children can imitate from watching television shows that are not edifying or even decent for that matter. Likewise, there are plenty of things adults can imitate too. Children are definitely porous. They are like sponges soaking up every bit of material that comes their way. That's why we have to be so careful. Just watch them. The way we fold our arms, put our hands in our pockets, laugh, eat (with our mouths open), refuse to sing in church, or scream at a ball game, it's all up for duplication by those who look up to us. Michael Jordan hit a nerve of American youth when his company coined the phrase, "Be like Mike!"

Adults, on the other hand, have built-in sensors created by maturity, wisdom, and knowledge. These attributes help dictate what we take in and what we spit out. Most adults have the ability to manage the material they are surrounded by. Yet, most of us are guilty of taking in what we should not and imitating behaviors unbecoming of a Christian. Even with the maturity, wisdom, and knowledge we have developed, we are porous, just like our children. That is why we need to fill our minds with that which is good and honorable. We should look to those who have gone before us, the spiritual leaders found in the Bible, to emulate and follow. Philippians 4:8 hits the nail on the head when Paul says, *Finally, brothers, whatever is true, whatever is noble, whatever is right, whatever is pure, whatever is lovely, whatever is admirable—if anything is excellent or praiseworthy—think about such things.*

Consider, for a moment, all that is promised during a political election. A presidential candidate, for example, can stand up in a debate and make various promises and claims, but it really doesn't matter what is said on the platform. What matters is the outcome of his conduct. The proof is in the pudding. How much more so as believers! My friend, it is not about what you and I say. It is not about making a public pronouncement. It is about imitating God by learning more about Him through the lives of others. So, how do we know who we should watch? Who we should imitate? Let's open our eyes and observe. Are they connected into the life of Jesus Christ who is the same yesterday, today, and forever? Is their conduct based on His unchanging nature? If so, they are worthy to be imitated.

#2—Put It into Practice

The writer of the letter to the Hebrews puts it like this: *Consider the outcome of their way of life and imitate their faith.* After we have studied their record and examined their conduct, we must put into practice what we've learned. Observation now becomes action. Why is this so important? It is important because it's the outward expression of our hearts. Our faith is the outward reflection of our relationship with God. When my heart is tied to God's, I'm able to put on the mind of Christ.

Using just two examples, one from the Old Testament and one from the New Testament, we are going to work through this together. I'm going to make an effort to show you how we can emulate leaders from the past and learn from them today. We will look at two of the spiritual giants mentioned in the Bible who are glowing examples of a life lived for God. We will make an effort to consider the outcome of their way of life and learn how to imitate their faith. The two men I want to examine are Job and Peter. Both of these guys had their share of struggles, as most great names in history do. Likewise, they both had their share of triumphs though when you think of major victories, neither of these men may come to mind. But I will show you that they were certainly victorious. They led lives which were pleasing to God, and so, we are able to follow in their footsteps.

Job. This man was tried in every way possible. I certainly do not envy him in any way. My goodness, can you imagine the hardships he endured? In the first chapter of the Book of Job, he lost his oxen, donkeys, sheep, servants, camels, more servants, sons, and daughters. And yet he still said, *"May the name of the LORD be praised."* What? Is he lucid? How can you go through all of that and come out saying, "Praise God"? Sounds pretty crazy, huh? Well, it wasn't really that cut and dry. He is not as crazy as he sounds; he wasn't skipping around whistling the hymn, "To God Be the Glory." Once Job had received all of this news, the text actually says in Job 1:20–22:

> *At this, Job got up and tore his robe and shaved his head. Then he fell to the ground in worship and said: "Naked I came from my mother's womb and naked I will depart. The LORD gave and the LORD has taken away; may the name of the LORD be praised." In all this, Job did not sin by charging God with wrongdoing.*

As we can clearly see, Job was not a happy camper. He was not pleased with his circumstances. In all reality, he was totally devastated.

I don't think I'm there yet, people. I have never experienced any-thing even close to what Job went through, but I could only imagine that if utter devastation came my way, I would want to point fingers at someone. I might even want to blame God for my loss. It is quite likely that I might sin in my heart or with my tongue if I lost all that Job had lost. Think about it, folks. This man is certainly worthy of imitation. I mean, how would you fare if you lost even a fourth of what Job did? Talk about a creditable spiritual leader. Beyond his ability to praise God despite his circumstances, his consistency, his loyalty, his righteousness, and the fact that he knew *all* he had belonged to God is proof plenty that he is a man of God, a man worth following. Notwithstanding his physical pain, his emotional turmoil, and his mental anguish, he never turned away from the face of God. Job 27:2–6 reads:

> *As surely as God lives, who has denied me justice, the Almighty, who has made me taste bitterness of soul, as long as I have life within me, the breath of God in my nostrils, my lips will not speak wickedness, and my tongue will utter no deceit. I will never admit you are in the right; till I die, I will not deny my integrity. I will maintain my righteousness and never let go of it; my conscience will not reproach me as long as I live.*

What an example! Despite all he endured, even the denial of jus-tice, Job refused to let go. What an incredible testimony! You see it's easy to praise God when your finances are in order, your kids are behav-ing nicely, and your spouse is being oh so sweet. But to praise God in the midst of turmoil and devastation—that's tough!

It's easy to see Job was a contented man. He praised God even when his own circumstances left him personally devastated. This is hard to do even at the best of times. How did he do this? A closer look at Job's re-sponse will help to put the right perspective on this matter. He wrestled with God. He was not pleased with what was going on. As a matter of fact, for twenty-some chapters, Job goes on and on about how *not* pleased he is. He didn't understand why God was allowing such pain in his life, and yet he clung to Him anyway. Do not misunderstand me here. Job never became discontent, for the Bible says he never sinned in his anger against God, but he did ask why and wonder when the pain was going to end.

It's like that story of the little boy who didn't listen to his dad. He had been told sternly and verbatim, "Do not cross the street." And yet, despite his father's instruction, he crossed the street. His father saw him, walked over to him and asked, "What do you think you're doing?" The little boy replied, "I had to go get my ball. It rolled across the street." He father did not care *why* his son had disobeyed him; the point was he disobeyed a very clear rule. Needless to say, the boy was in major trouble. All the way back over to his house, the little boy clung to his father's leg, saying, "I don't like you. I think you are mean. You're not my friend anymore." The son knew he was about to get in trouble, and he still held on to the one person whom he trusted—Daddy.

This is just what Job did. He went to God and shook on His leg. He cried in His arms asking, "Why are You allowing this?" I think this shows ultimate intimacy with God. The only person Job wanted to run to and share his pain with was the same person allowing this pain to occur in the first place. Job recognized the power of God, but with the same breath he knew the security of God. Job knew he could shake the tree and that the tree wouldn't fall down. God could handle it then, and He can handle it now. He is the same yesterday, today, and tomorrow. God wants to hear about it. He doesn't want us to run and tell someone else about our hurts and pains; He wants to know. This, my friend, is something to imitate. Try telling God your problems, your pains, and your desires. He knows what they are anyway. Take a lesson from Job and let God be your safe place to shake.

I do believe I have met a modern-day Job. He would not consider himself as such, but I do. No, I am not suggesting this man suffered to the same extent as Job, but I would love to be able to set the limit or extent of loss it takes to qualify a person as a modern-day Job. Melvin Parker is not only my friend, but he is one of the dearest men of God I have ever met in my life. His wife, Ellen, a precious, godly lady of the highest order became stricken with cancer. How we prayed with her and for her, but our Savior chose to call her home. She crossed the finish line in triumph, having lived her life well and pleasing to our Savior. Melvin's heart was broken, but his spirit rejoiced in the knowledge he would himself cross the finish line and be reunited with her in heaven one day. If the passing of Ellen was not enough for one man to bear, I shall never forget the phone call I received from Melvin some months later. I charged over to his home where my friend was standing in the bedroom of his oldest son, Mel, Jr. His son had gone to sleep and had suddenly died right there. Melvin's heart was broken for he had now lost his oldest son. But his life was to be shattered again when his youngest granddaughter, Tory, was tragically killed, along with her thirteen-year-old friend, in a car accident on an icy road in South Carolina. I will never forget conducting that funeral with Tory's dad, David, and her grandfather, Melvin, sitting there in a state of unmitigated shock and grief. But here's the bottom line. To this day, Melvin Parker (now married to precious Carol), has carried and conducted himself with a grace and refinement that can only come from the Lord Jesus. A sweeter, more giving spirit is hard to find!

Simon Peter. He was an early disciple of Jesus who was present at the very first miracle recorded in the New Testament. He was there when Jesus turned the water into wine at the wedding in Cana of Galilee. Peter was a fisherman by trade but followed the call of Christ and became a "fisher of men." Peter was a zealous guy. Even as I sit here and write about him, a smile creeps across my face. He must have been one of the more enthusiastic men of the bunch. I would have enjoyed being around him. Scriptures depict a man who was almost childlike in his zeal. His enthusiasm got him in trouble more than once. You can bet that Peter was often the one sticking his foot in his mouth, not with any ill intention, just curiously and stubbornly loyal to Christ. It is evident that he was very special to Jesus and he was quite prominent among the disciples.

As with Job, Satan asked for Peter. He wanted to put Peter to the test. The Scriptures are strangely similar. Luke 22:31–32, states:

Simon, Simon, Satan has asked to sift you as wheat. But I have prayed for you, Simon, that your faith may not fail. And when you have turned back, strengthen your brothers.

Likewise, Job 1:9–12, reads:

"Does Job fear God for nothing?" Satan replied. "Have you not put a hedge around him and his household and everything he has? You have blessed the work of his hands, so that his flocks and herds are spread throughout the land. But stretch out your hand and strike everything he has, and he will surely curse you to your face." The LORD said to Satan, "Very well, then, everything he has is in your hands, but on the man himself do not lay a finger." Then Satan went out from the presence of the LORD.

Peter, like Job, was apparently a strong enough fellow in his faith for God to say, "Satan, it's okay to test him. He can handle it because his faith is grounded in Me." Well, Simon Peter didn't exactly come through with flying colors on this one. Just as Jesus told him at the Last Supper, Peter denied even knowing him, not once, not twice, but three times! Verses 33–34 of Luke 22 state, *"But he replied, 'Lord, I am ready to go with you to prison and to death.' Jesus answered, 'I tell you, Peter, before the rooster crows today, you will deny three times that you know me.'"* Jesus knew all the while that Peter was going to fail. But let's look at what Christ told him just moments earlier. *And when you have turned back, strengthen your brothers* (Luke 22:32). Jesus is saying, "I know you are going to mess up, though you can't fathom it right now. It's okay, just turn back and keep pressing forward."

I want you to understand something really important here. Although Peter vehemently denied knowing Christ, Satan still was not victorious. Satan was trying to fail Peter's faith. He wanted to "sift" him. Satan set out to destroy his faith; to make him so weak and frail that he couldn't go on. That's exactly what some of us do. Instead of running to God and grabbing hold of His leg in a desperate attempt to garner His support and strength, we turn, run, and hide. This is a dangerous place to be. This is where faith is lost. Peter, like Job, understood that. Yes, Peter denied Christ, not once, not twice, but three times. But what did he do afterwards? He turned back and strengthened his brothers. Do not let this point be lost. Peter's faith was not torn; he did not fall into Satan's hands despite his desperate state.

Do you recall the time Peter walked on water? We read about this remarkable event in Matthew 14. It took place immediately following the feeding of the five thousand, and the disciples did not understand what had just happened. In Mark's text, it even says that their hearts were hardened because they did not understand about the loaves (Mark 6:51). Jesus had told the disciples to go on without Him while He dismissed the crowd and went on a hillside to pray. Night was falling, and the disciples' boat was a considerable distance away. Verses 25–31 read:

> *"During the fourth watch of the night Jesus went out to them, walking on the lake. When the disciples saw him walking on the lake, they were terrified. "It's a ghost,' they said, and cried out in fear. But Jesus immediately said to them, 'Take courage! It is I. Don't be afraid."* (And here comes the Simon Peter we all know and love . . .) *?Lord, if it's you,' Peter replied, 'Tell me to come to you on the water.' 'Come,' He said. Then Peter got down out*

*of the boat, walked on the water and came toward Jesus. But
when he saw the wind, he was afraid and, beginning to sink,
cried out, 'Lord, save me!' Immediately Jesus reached out his
hand and caught him. 'You of little faith,' He said, 'Why did you
doubt?'"*

Now, I know he fell, both literally and figuratively. But do you
know what he did do? He had the guts to say, "Lord, if that really is you,
I know you can do anything, so let me walk on water too." It's almost
like he's trying to call a bluff, perhaps because the disciples thought they
were looking at an apparition or ghost coming towards them on the water. Peter, however, persisted and might have thought, "This will show
him. You can't go around claiming to be my Jesus. I'll call you on it."
And that's just what happened. Peter hopped right out of the boat and
walked on water. Whether he was calling "the ghost's" bluff or he was
so passionate that he didn't waste time on logic, he stepped out of the
boat. That is a big deal, folks. Just hold it right there. He stepped out
of the boat. That is a glimpse of the character of Peter. Do you find
yourself stepping out in faith like that? Phew, Peter certainly puts me in
my place. I don't know if I would have the nerve to step out when the
entire endeavor is humanly and practically impossible. But that's just
what he did. He had faith. Yes, he became distracted by the winds and
the waves, but he took a step of faith. He put it all in God's hands. Even
at his greatest moment of terror and desperation, Peter looks back
squarely into the face of the one who gave him the courage to step out
of the boat to begin with. The Lord Jesus Christ! Like Job, Peter appeared to understand that the courage to step out of the boat, the power
to walk on the water, and the ability to prevent him from drowning all
came from only one source. This is quite remarkable really. If I am going to imitate someone, I believe I am going to be well inclined to follow the leadership of someone like Peter. The three ingredients of
courage, power, and ability are so critical as we run the race of life. I

want to be like Peter, don't you? We will never know what we can do until we put our faith and trust in Christ.

By taking these two examples of spiritual leaders, observing their conduct, and examining their lives, we are able to put into practice the lessons these men have taught us. Job was steadfast and strong in his faith. He understood that God was in charge. No matter how bad his earthly circumstances became, neither his character nor his faith were ever affected. Peter, on the other hand, loved the Lord fearlessly. He stood right by His side. But he made mistakes (the kind of mistakes we turn into Sunday school object lessons). Regardless of his shortcomings, he never allowed his mistakes to diminish his faith. He just kept coming back for more. These men were so solid in their faith that God actually allowed Satan to test them and sift them. Wow! What examples to follow and what lives to emulate. Perhaps the writer to the Hebrews had these two men in mind when he admonished his readers to imitate another's faith.

One of the marks of a true believer is a God-given ability to keep going despite the many pitfalls life has to offer. All of us have been there at one time or another. Perhaps this is why men such as Peter and Job are worth imitating. Even when great leaders like Job and Peter messed up, even when they were put in situations that seemed hopeless, they relied on God for their strength and refuge. Like us, these men fell down and stumbled during the race of life. But whether they were knocked down by circumstances, rolling waves, fear, or desperation, they struggled back up and kept on running toward the finish line. We, too, must do the same. We've got to keep running; it is imperative to "keep on truckin'" toward the finish line. Jesus is waiting there for us.

Imitation just may be at the heart of your greatest problem. Life has become too insular. You are moving toward the finish line solo. You need help. Open your eyes. Look around. It's really amazing the people who surround us, precious people with all kinds of giftedness and capabilities, people who just seem to have it right. You and I know who they are. They stand out. They are sought after. God has placed them there for you and me. Imitate the great leaders of our faith. Watch how they do things. Take note of their attitudes. Write them on the tablets of your heart. And, above all else, "let this mind be in you which was also in Christ Jesus." Even the best of the best will let you down. So, do not ever hero worship or place man on a higher plane than he is capable of being on. Take what is good and discard that which is bad. Then look to our Savior in all things. And you and I will finish well!

THE NINTH CHAPTER

To Know the Truth

See to it that no one takes you captive through hollow and deceptive philosophy, which depends on human tradition and the basic principles of this world rather than on Christ.

—Colossians 2:8

Scripture Reference: Hebrews 13:9
Do not be carried away by all kinds of strange teachings.
It is good for our hearts to be strengthened by grace, not by ceremonial foods, which are of no value to those who eat them.

True\'tru\adj **1 a:** steadfast, loyal **b:** honest, just **2 a:** being in accordance with the actual state of affairs **b:** ideal, essential **c:** being that which is the case rather than that which is manifest or assumed.

False\'fols\adj **1 a:** not genuine **2 a:** intentionally untrue **b:** adjusted or made so as to deceive.

Knowing what is true and recognizing what is false is a critical element in our lives. We rely upon truth to make decisions, to determine our creeds, and to guide our thinking. Truth is the basis for what we do and how we do it. Think about it. We apply the absolutes of truth to just about everything we do and everything we hold dear. If it's true that it is raining, we take an umbrella. If it's true that the light is green, we go. We base our actions on the truth of the matter from small, simple things to large, consequential issues.

Dan Brown's novel, *The DaVinci Code*, sold millions of copies. The movie by the same name has sparked untold debate. A furor erupted across the world over the claims that Jesus was married to Mary Magdalene, who bore Him a child by the name of Sarah. According to Brown, Mary was pregnant at the foot of the cross. Due to fear, she fled for her life to France, then known as Gaul. There she took refuge in a Jewish sect and delivered her daughter, who became God's appointed bloodline to this day. There are numerous other contentions made by Brown through his characters and the story line. An organization known as The Priory of Sion was formed with the specific purpose of protecting Jesus' bloodline through Mary, uncovering the great secret and revealing it at the appointed hour. This secret group also appointed the Knights Templar, who were assigned the responsibility of protecting the secret as a kind of "musketeer" force. The organization which opposed the secret was known as the *Opus Dei*, and the members were seen as the antagonists. The Roman Catholic Church supposedly was their greatest supporter. Leonardo DaVinci's depiction of the Last Supper evidently proved the presence of Mary and her relationship with Jesus. Works other than the Bible, such as the *Gospel of Phillip* and others, were evidence of the feminization of the godhead and the need for God to have a female divine placed alongside Himself. The Emperor Constantine's convening of the Council of Nicaea in A.D. 325. was politically motivated. In order to improve his popularity with the people, Constantine collated the Bible as we have it today, eliminated goddess worship, and decreed the divine nature of Jesus Christ as God. (I would encourage you to order the full text of the May 7, 2006, message I preached on *The Encouraging Word*. The message was titled: "The DaVinci Code: A Christian Response.")

Here's the issue: how do we determine what is fact and what is fantasy?

And is this really important? Some have suggested the Christian world ought to be silent. Others have suggested it is time to launch the new crusade! The bottom line is the issue of being strong and staying strong, even in difficult times. The Bible teaches, *Then you will know the truth, and the truth will set you free* (John 8:32). If we are to reach the finish line well, and to run the journey of life with strength and courage, then we must know the truth.

There are numerous definitions of truth; the dictionary abounds with explanations. There are also different disciplines which utilize this concept: logic, religion, politics, law, and mathematics. There are different types of truth: objective, subjective, relative, and absolute. There are even varying theories on truth: the semantic theory of truth, Kripke's theory of truth, and the redundancy theory all state their cases with much articulation and expression. Needless to say, literature on the matter of truth is in great supply. Let's look at how logic employs this notion, for example. An argument is valid if it cannot lead from a true premise to a false conclusion: *All As are Bs; some Bs are Cs; therefore, some As are Cs.* In the discipline of law, individuals who testify are sworn to "tell the truth, the whole truth, and nothing but the truth." They are not expected to make infallibly true statements, void of any falsehoods; rather they are making a good-faith attempt to recount events, etc., as they remember them to be. The truth is all around us in some form or another. Knowing the truth and how it applies to each and every situation, therefore, is necessary in order for us to make wise decisions and live a highly functioning life.

So I ask you, with all this truth floating around, how do we know what to believe? Which truth is really true and which "truth" is false? How can we decipher between a "good-sounding" falsehood and a "difficult-to-swallow" truth? Which theory do you buy into; what religious truth do you follow? We will make every effort to provide some answers to these important questions as this chapter unfolds. The idea of truth can be as philosophical as we want to make it, but I don't want to make it as such. The real truth is not complex, complicated, or entailed. It is straightforward, narrow, and exact. It is also sitting right before us. God's Word is the only form of truth we can believe in one hundred percent. We don't have to concern ourselves with applying the redundancy theory or deciding if A+B=C. We only have to read and study His Word. Now, don't get me wrong here. I'm all for digging in and learning about the definitions, disciplines, types, and theories of truth. Go for it! What I am saying is this: we don't have to do all of that. We don't have to understand what the world believes truth to be because we already have the information at our disposal. It's all written down in the Word of God.

Let's take our next verse for example. Hebrews 13:9 reads, *"Do not be carried away by all kinds of strange teachings. It is good for our hearts to be strengthened by grace, not by ceremonial foods, which are of no value to those who eat them."* Now, why would we be reminded to "not be carried away by false teachings"? Perhaps it is because the writer had seen it happen; he had seen believers swept away. Even in our day and age, this has become more and more of a problem among many of our students. So many of them are fortunate enough to grow up in loving Christian homes, go off to the colleges of their choice, and yet come back with heads full of garbage. This is another reason why we have a responsibility to teach our young people the essential meaning of truth. It has become increasingly imperative to sit our youth down and say something along these lines: "I know you are going to meet people who believe differently than you do. Just remember, when you're faced with philosophies, religions, and ideas that are contrary to yours, stand firm in what you know to be absolute truth." Parents, they've got to hear this from you. We must teach our children to base their beliefs in the Word of God, to ground them in Christ. If we do this, then the winds that blow will not carry us away.

In this verse in Hebrews, we are warned to beware of false teachings; to stand firm in what we know to be true. Beyond that, we are also encouraged to find strength in God's grace, not allowing ourselves to be further swept away by the ceremonial mumbo-jumbo that can sometimes overtake us. We have all been guilty of this, getting caught up in our godly to-do lists:

1. Take my Bible to church.
2. Sing in the choir.
3. Join a Sunday school class.
4. Have a quiet time.
5. Pray before meals.

Sounds pretty familiar, huh? Not only are we warned about succumbing to false teachings, but we are also warned about developing a ceremonial belief in God. The author wants us to find hope, find faith in God's grace, not in works or pharisaical ways. If we allow ourselves to be carried away by our ceremonies, our faith will become false. It won't really be "faith"; it will be works.

So, how can we take heed of these warnings and pinpoint false teaching when we see or hear one? How do we tell a truth from a lie? Some believe that in order to discern false teachings from true ones, we must learn more about them. I agree with this, to a certain extent. I think it's relevant and worthy of study to examine other teachings and religions in order to understand what they believe and why they believe it. Furthermore, I think this is of benefit because, in some cases, it shows us to an even greater extent what we believe; it solidifies our faith. However, studying and learning more about Mormonism, Buddhism, Scientology, or the Jehovah's Witness sect can prove to be problematic if your own faith isn't as strong as it should be. It's like treading on thin ice—you just might fall in!

It has been said, "You are what you believe." I submit this can be taken even further. "What you believe will determine how you live." Just take a look back at the 1980s in the United States of America.

These were some of the darkest days ever for the evangelical church. The stage was occupied by some well-known, highly gifted television preachers. Each had his own unique niche, his own unique style, his own unique set of followers, and his own unique set of beliefs. Without taking anything away from the scores of deeply spiritual men and women out there, it was a sad day when a few of these self-styled champions of the Christian faith began to fall like dominoes. I believe the core of their problems was the fundamental basis of what they believed. Their opinion was placed on a much higher plane than the Word of God, so much so that advice and counsel were hardly sought nor desired, even when one of them had succumbed to temptation and lust. One of them even made an announcement that God had appeared to him in a dream and had given him a vision that he (the evangelist) was the (only) one God had decided to use to reach America for Jesus Christ. Quite a claim when one thinks about it. The church still suffers to this day, and one will never truly know just how many thousands of lives were lost for Christ because of the ruined witness of just a few.

Hebrews 11 is widely known as the "hall of faith" because it recounts the dramatic manner with which many of God's great servants served Him with a radical faith. My personal favorite has always been Moses. Here was a man who had grown up as the son of Pharaoh's daughter. Talk about a silver spoon in his mouth! I saw a show on television recently that dealt with the lives of the richest people on earth. The Sultan of Brunei is reputedly one of the wealthiest men in the world, and his lavish palaces and lifestyle certainly reflect it. But it has been said that Pharaoh's riches would cause even the sultan's billions to pale in comparison. Such was the heritage of Moses. And yet he left Egypt. A closer look reveals the reason why he left Egypt. It was because he believed the truth about God. He saw that which was invisible. He was a man of absolute conviction. And he acted on it.

Abraham was no different than Moses. In Genesis 12:1–4, we read of the stark truth of the stark action of a man who understood what he heard and believed what he heard and did what he believed. God spoke to him in a clear and direct manner, telling him that He would be with Abram through thick and through thin so long as he believed what he heard and then did what he believed. I love verse four because it smacks every person desirous of serving the Lord in the heart. God spoke and Abram departed as the Lord had spoken to him. If you really want to understand the significance of this, consider the context of God's instruction to His servant. Abram was, in all likelihood, a very wealthy man. God told him to get up and go to a land that He had yet to reveal to His servant. Abram acted without even knowing where he was going or what he would find when he arrived wherever it was he was going to go. He most certainly heard God telling him he would be blessed beyond his imagination. He heard God laying out a future that must have been literally unbelievable. But how could Abram ever have understood the meaning of "father of many nations" when he didn't even have one child of his own to begin with? Such was the magnificence of his faith as he gathered his tribe together and set out for a distant land he had never been to before.

Do you have a similar story to report? It happened to my wife, Karyn, and me many years ago. Both of us, recently married, were doing very well as teachers. The future looked bright indeed. I had just been promoted and, to make matters even more the sweeter, I was a finalist for a major scholarship to earn a Ph.D. at an institution overseas of my own choosing. I applied and was accepted in Australia, the United States, England, and Scotland, but God had another plan for my life. God sent a pastor by the name of J. Roy McComb from Columbia, Mississippi, all the way to my home in Africa to bring a special word to me from the Lord. Both Karyn and I knew God was speaking to us through J. Roy and Chester Vaughn, from Jackson, Mississippi. Within three short months, we had resigned our careers and sold all our worldly possessions in order to pay off government debts for education and buy tickets to fly to the United States of America. We landed in New York City, literally not knowing what we were doing or where we were exactly—and with only $1,400 in our pockets. We left behind all our friends and every frame of reference. We arrived with nothing, not knowing anybody, with no idea of the future. Within a few short months, we became the recipients of more acts of kindness and love than we could ever imagine. Today, by the grace and mercy of the Lord Jesus Christ, we have the privilege of counting more friends than we could have ever imagined, teaching at colleges and seminaries I had never heard of, rubbing shoulders with presidents and people I only dreamed about. We've had the opportunity of pastoring wonderful churches, filled with precious people, traveling literally around the world to share the good news about Jesus, writing books and preaching now to millions across our nation, being loved by the most beautiful woman I have ever been around, and being called Dad by those who are closest to my heart. I have a house to live in with a deck to sit on, tea to drink, cars to drive, and a dog named Bully. What more could a man ask for?

Therefore, I think it's most prudent to learn more about what you believe, to learn more about your own faith so you can spot those teachings which are different or that challenge your own. Let's look briefly at how we can do this. Perhaps I could make a few helpful suggestions in this regard. I want to show you how to spot a falsehood by knowing the truth. I have broken it down into three easy-to-follow steps: Test, Seek, and Pray.

#1—Test

You've got to be put to the test. When you are faced with a situation, a decision, a teaching, or a philosophy that leaves you questioning its validity or truth, ask yourself these questions:

1. Is it scripturally sound?
2. Does it go against the Word of God in any way?
3. Will it cause me to compromise my Christian witness?
4. Is it counter to my common sense and past experiences?
5. Will it bring strife to my life, my friends, or my family?

Answering these questions will yield a yes or no answer: Yes, it is true or, no, it is false. There should be no maybes when you do this—it either goes against the Word of God or it doesn't. Don't make it more complicated than it has to be. God's way is not hidden from us. It is laid out in black and white. You will be able to determine if the thing in question is true or false by testing first. Remember "when in doubt, leave out"! God will never cause you to compromise. And His Holy Spirit always gives you peace.

#2—Seek

You've got to seek wise counsel. Speak to your pastor, read a book, talk to a friend; find godly guidance. (I want to qualify this by saying that the pastor, the book, and the friend you choose to seek should all be godly examples. Please do not look to someone who will tickle your ears and tell you just what you want to hear.) Your church, your friends, this book you are reading right now are all resources to utilize. If an idea, concept, or philosophy comes your way and you're not sure what to make of it, seek counsel from someone who is after God's own heart. They will have wise advice because they are attuned to God's voice and they know His Word.

#3—Pray

You've got to pray about it. If you have a right relationship with God, and you pray to Him daily, our heavenly Father will help you discern right from wrong. Herein lies the beauty of prayer. Simply put, prayer is communication with God. If we communicate with Him often, we will get to know Him. We will learn His likes, His dislikes, what pleases Him, and what saddens Him. It's just like meeting new friends. Initially, you know very little about them. They have brown hair; they are six feet tall, etc., etc. It takes some time to really get to know others, does it not? The more conversations you are able to have with them, the more you get to know one another. Just watch a couple who begin the dating game. They meet and are introduced to one another. Then the cell phone begins to work overtime. Then the outings and the conversations. One question follows another. Gradually, something very special begins to happen. They fall in love! A similar parallel can be drawn in our relationship with our Savior. If you pray and have an ongoing, vital prayer life with your Savior, you will develop a keen sense of truth; you will become discerning. When false teachings rear their ugly heads or even a sweet-sounding falsehood makes you question what you believe, you will know the right thing to do because your trust, faith, and belief is in the Lord Jesus Christ.

So, we have determined thus far some of the ways in which we can detect false teachings. First, we test it against the Word of God, then we seek wise, godly counsel, and, finally, we pray about it. Whenever teachings that are questionable come to us, those three steps will help guide us through. Now I want to look at how we can better know the truth, how we can grow stronger in our faith so falsehoods won't confuse us or sway us. I want to examine how being more grounded in the Word of God will better equip us to differentiate between that which is of the Lord and that which is not. In order to help us get a better handle on this somewhat difficult subject, I have broken it down into a suggested plan of action. These three ways can help us grow as Christians and equip us to be ready to recognize, refute, and resolve false teachings.

Action #1: Study Hard

Most of us would agree there are no shortcuts in this life. If something is worth having, it's worth earning. Shortcuts serve little purpose anyway. In order to be strong in your faith, you must study hard. Do not compromise; do not take the easy way out. Life involves hard work. As a Christian person, you have a mandate to study; you have a mandate to understand God's will and His Word. Put your hand to the plow; be willing to pay the price. Be determined and don't give up. Do not take shortcuts in life and see how little you can get by with. Find God's path for you by studying His Word. If you are going to be strong when the winds blow, you must study hard. Be diligent so that when race time comes, you will be prepared and ready to run.

Action #2: Step Out

Let me give you an illustration that affects all of us in one way or another. Every stage and every phase of life offers new and varied challenges. Consider, for example, our college students. I love them so much. What can we say that would help them during this exciting time of life? How can they step out strong and be strong in the challenging contexts in which many of them find themselves on our college campuses? I realize this is easier said than done, but I remain convinced in my heart they need to step out and stand up without apology. It's kind of similar to the friend who asked me to pray with him about his addiction to cigarettes. He asked me to help him quit the habit that was slowly killing him. I guess the look on his face spoke volumes when I told him he simply needed to lay those "cancer sticks" down and walk away from them. I told him he would go through two or three weeks of untold misery. He would feel as though he was about to die! He would find himself trying to get any "whiff" of second-hand smoke he could find. But I also told him that three weeks of withdrawal and pain was far better than the alternative. Believe it or not, he stepped out and did exactly what I had suggested to him. Today he is a free man. And so my rather radical advice to our students: If you know who you are and who you serve, then don't mess around with the things that will bring you down. Is it too radical to suggest that a college student simply say, "No, I don't do that. I don't care about being popular. I don't care if I'm not accepted into your sorority or fraternity. I march according to *this* drumbeat. I want you to know that I am who I am by the grace of God"? Now, that is stepping out strong! But I know many of you are sitting there saying, "With all due respect, that's not very realistic, pastor. Teenagers are way too concerned with what others think of them to come right out and say that to their peers."

A television talk show host I actually enjoy listening to really had it wrong with a comment he made on one of his shows. The subject dealt with the problem of teenage drinking of alcohol, especially during spring break and graduation blowouts at the beach. The question raised the issue of how to curb the devastation in the lives of so many as a result of these binges, including unwanted pregnancies, alcoholism, prison records, and ruined lives. The discussion was heated and spirited, as it usually is on these shows where everyone has an opinion and no one listens to another's opinion. What troubled me was the host, a man of great influence, actually said, "Ah, come on! Let's face it. They are going to drink whether we like it or not. The question is how can we teach them to know when to stop?" Can you believe this? I may be considered the most out-of-touch, old-fashioned individual in the world, but I still believe that what you know to be true will govern how you behave. I have met many fine young people who have just said no. If we can spend millions on advertising that insists our youth say no to drugs, what do we think alcohol is? Surely someone is going to wake up and be honest about this!

In order to finish strong, let's not throw up our arms in despair.

Conviction still counts. There is so much we can still do for ourselves and for those we love. We can still step out strong. High school students, college students, and even we, as parents, can communicate that we are different, that we stand for something, by what we say, by what we don't say, by what we do, and by what we don't do.

Teens, as well as adults, do not have to be extreme when they are stepping out. Teenagers do not have to make a public announcement when they enter Biology 101, "I'm here. I'm a Christian, and I don't care what you think." Likewise, adults do not have to recite Scripture from atop their cubicles, "This is what John 3:16 says to me . . ." Stepping out strong requires that we let others know what we believe, what we stand for. This can be done by not laughing at a cruel or inappropriate joke, by praying before you eat lunch, by not using bad language when everyone around you is, by working God into the conversation at the water cooler, by going to church on Sunday and letting others hear about it on Monday. Determine who you are, and then live like it. Set your standards according to the Word of God and do not compromise. Step out strong so others will know what you believe and why you believe it.

Action #3: Stand Up

Sometimes we are faced with circumstances, whether it is a false teaching or just a tough situation, when we are forced to stand up and stand against something. This is usually not a very comfortable position to be in. Typically, I would say in almost every case, we will ruffle a few feathers. And most of us are not comfortable doing this. We like to keep the boat nice and steady. Say a coworker tells an off-color joke and you know you should say something; you know you should stand up. But you think, "Oh, God, please don't make me rock the boat. I don't want to cause any trouble here." Well, being a Christian means that from time to time we will have to be vocal. In some cases, it's not enough to simply refuse to laugh at the joke. Rather, we have to say something; we have to be a light.

We all know what light does in a room full of darkness? It illuminates what's there. In a darkened world, it is our responsibility to shine the light so others can see Jesus. Now, this doesn't mean carrying a stick around beating others in the head yelling, "You're doing that wrong. You're being bad." Friend, we are all sinners—every last one of us. It is not for us to judge anyone, lest we be judged. But in some cases we have to stand up for what we know to be true. And we do so in a loving manner. The goal is not to point out the bad but to highlight the good. It just so happens the closer we get to the light, the more the darkness is revealed. We've got to stand up for our faith, our beliefs, and our values so others can see the light.

When you study hard, step out strong, and stand up for what you believe, you should be prepared for possible worldly consequences. You might not be popular; you might not get to hear what everyone is laughing at around the water cooler; you might not be asked to go to the party. But that's okay. It's actually great because you have communicated to your peers that being swept up by the false lusts of life isn't for you. You have stood up and stepped out. You have become bold and resolute. I promise it will get easier to let others know *where* you stand and *who* you stand for. It may take some time, but it will definitely be worth the while. And pretty soon, others will know it isn't a good idea to tell that joke in front of you or to use bad language while you're around. You'll be a light shining God's presence into the lives of those you encounter. Take heart when this portion of the race gets tough because it's not an easy path to choose. Often, people run and hide from the light. John 3:19–21 has a good concluding word on this subject:

> *This is the verdict: Light has come into the world, but men loved darkness instead of light because their deeds were evil. Everyone*

who does evil hates the light, and will not come into the light for
fear that his deeds will be exposed. But whoever lives by the truth
comes into the light, so that it may be seen plainly that what he
has done has been done through God.

I don't know about you, but I want to be popular with God. It doesn't make any difference to me if I'm popular with the world. I'm standing in line for the grace of God, and I want God to bless me. I want His Spirit poured out on me. In America today, in our churches today, there ought to be people who are willing to stand up and be counted for righteousness. I want to be a part of that group. I want it to make a difference that I lived on this earth. When I enter the gates of heaven, I want my Father to say, "Well done, my child."

It seems to me that our Savior looks into the hearts of all those He loves and encourages them to be strong and take courage. The race of life is so difficult, even at the best of times. Strange teachings will assuredly come our way. It may be as obvious as the nose on our face, or it could be as subtle as a whisper in our ear. Either way, we have to know the truth; we have to be able to spot a falsehood by being grounded in the Word of God. If we are ever faced with a questionable situation, we test, seek, and pray to find the will of God. Then we can take action. We can study hard, step out strong, and stand up straight so we can be a beacon of light for our Lord Jesus Christ.

Would it not be great if we developed a new way of saying good-bye to one another at the end of a wonderful family time together during the holidays? Think about this. Perhaps your grown children have all been home for the holidays and you and your spouse are standing, tearfully, at the front door with mixed emotions. Glad they came. Glad you had such a happy time. Glad they are doing so well. But equally glad to know you will have the TV to yourself, actually be able to sit down and not say one word if you don't feel like it. And glad that the grandkids are going home with their parents and are not going to stay with Okie and Dokie for another "few days," so Dokie can take them to the fun park again.

Would it not be great if the new American benediction was, "We'll see you at the finish line!"

THE TENTH CHAPTER

A Relationship of Praise

Great is the LORD and most worthy of praise; his greatness no one can fathom.

—Psalm 145:3

Scripture Reference: Hebrews 13:15–16
*Through Jesus, therefore, let us continually offer to God
a sacrifice of praise—the fruit of lips that confess his name.
And do not forget to do good and to share with others,
for with such sacrifices God is pleased.*

Do you know why you and I were put on this earth? Believe it or not, it wasn't so we could have a family, be successful, or accumulate material possessions. The hand of God put us here so we could praise His name. That's it, pure and simple. All the other things of this world which become blessings to us are only glimpses into His glories. When God created man, when He first lifted Adam from the dust, and when He first breathed the breath of life into Eve, His desire was to have a relationship with man. God has put us here for one purpose: to have a relationship of praise with Him.

One of the greatest ironies of our culture is our undeniable capacity to praise everything and anything with great gusto, yet when it comes to our praise of God we undergo a metamorphosis too strange to contemplate. Consider the football game. I, too, love football. Observe with me, if you please, the average American football fan. I am fully acquainted with grown men who spend an entire week in preparation for the big game on Saturday. Everything they do, from constant discussion and analysis to the minute details of personal and family preparation, is geared toward the event. Saturday morning begins bright and early with more than a song in the heart. Usually the "war song" thunders through the house like a freight train honking its deafening horn at a dangerous crossing. The children are amazed at Dad's high-spirited antics and his total willingness to be silly. The vehicle is packed with meticulous care, and the family sets off with a song in their hearts. Game day has arrived. Same as last week and the week before and the week before. Their reserved spot is where it always is, and the neighboring reserved spots are already filled with all the friends and familiar faces. They stopped en route and bought up all the remaining chicken at the local fried chicken franchise, sparing no cost whatever. They even added the extras just in case of an emergency. And, by the way, they arrived five hours before kickoff so as to practice their praise songs to the max!

When the whistle blows to signal the start of the rivals' long-awaited game, Dad can be seen quite clearly and distinctly. He's the one wearing all the colors of the home team from head to toe. In his hands, he carries a flag. On his head sits a cross between a pom-pom and the remains of a fluffy bird of sorts. This man hoots and hollers throughout the game. He sings the war song with all of his heart and waves his flag without reserve for the entire game. Money is no object or hindrance. He buys this and he buys that, never questioning the exorbitant prices, and is even generous to those seated around him. The game finally ends and high fives are handed out all the way down the winding, concrete walkway and back to the reserved spot where the crowd of fans gathers once again for a final two hours of singing, worship, and praise for the referees, the coach, and even the quarterback, whose "quarterback sneak" stole the game from the highly ranked gangsters who showed up and tried to take "us" on in "our" own backyard!

The next morning arrives far too early at 9:30 a.m. Mother insists they all get dressed and go to church. The reluctance with which Dad approaches his boiled eggs is only a foretaste of what lies ahead. "Come on, kids," he bemoans with an enthusiasm that would put an entire stadium to sleep in ten seconds. With great fervor the family arrives in the parking lot and immediately begins to complain about how far they have to walk to get to church. One person after another passes them by. They greet their recognizable friends and pat each other on the back in praise of the gallant effort of "our" team yesterday. Every now and then some unfortunate recognizable friend passes by whose misfortune it was to be a fan of the "other" team. "Tough day, huh?" Dad points out. Needless to say, several strangers pass him by. One on the left and one on the right. They look new. They look lost. They are just looking. Seeking. But this dad makes no move to smile at them. He makes no effort to greet them. He hardly even looks at them. The worship center is either too hot or too cold. The seats are their usual "too hard." The woman in front with the hat on makes him so mad he could bite her head off, and the kid who keeps fidgeting, well! The minister of music stands and smiles and announces the first hymn. "It is so good to be in the house of the Lord this morning. Let's stand and sing 'Victory in Jesus' with all of our hearts." The same man who just a few hours ago was willing to go berserk in his praise for a football team stands with great reluctance to his feet. But he doesn't open his mouth. And his countenance looks like he is recovering from hookworm treatment!

And his children are watching him.

When you hear the word "praise," what comes to mind? Do you automatically think of a hymn or a chorus you love to sing in church, maybe a praise song swells up in your heart? Perhaps your thoughts turn to the times you heaped praise on your son or daughter. "Way to go, little buddy!" Or maybe you think about commending someone for a job well done, "You did an excellent job. Thank you for your dedication." Praise *can* be all those things. But in this case, I suggest we consider this in terms of worship.

Any perspective considered will ultimately lead to a consideration of praise as an act of worship. As such, it is an action; it is something we do in response to God. It is an acted-out activity which is practically directed toward our Savior. Did you get that? It is not a passive term—it's a verb. It requires action to make it so. Therefore, we must make an effort to praise God. It won't just happen if we aren't deliberate about it. In Hebrews 13:15–16, Christians are encouraged to *"offer to God a sacrifice of praise—the fruit of lips that confess His name."* A closer analysis of the meaning of this directive reveals two considerations.

Number one: Our sacrifice is to praise God. This is one of the primary requests God makes of mankind. Think about it for a moment. My goodness, if that's all the Creator of the universe wants from me, how can I refuse, forget, or deny Him that request? He's not asking for a perfect lamb to be sacrificed on an altar or even a ceremonial burnt offering to be made. He is asking for our praise. The mandate to praise God shouldn't be much of a sacrifice anyway for those of us who love the Lord Jesus Christ. It should just be who we are and what we want to do. But we must remember, at the same time, that sacrifice implies the giving up of something. Surely it carries with it the idea of putting ourselves out for God. In other words, we praise the Lord, even when we do not "feel" like it.

Number two: Our praise should be the fruit of our lips. I want to take this one a step farther and say our praise should be the fruit of our hearts. You see, what comes out of our mouths started in our hearts. Matthew 12:34 states, *"For out of the overflow of the heart the mouth speaks."* Our praise for God originates in our hearts. If the heart isn't in the right place, praising God will not come easily. So, in order to fulfill this supplication, we must give God the sacrifice He so deserves, which is our praise. That praise should be the fruit of a heart filled with gratitude and thanksgiving for all our Savior has done for us.

My wife and I love gardens. Every time we go to England or Canada or beautiful South Africa, we are struck by the magnificence of the flowers. South Carolina is a flower-rich state as is most of the United States of America. Every year, Karyn busies herself about the flower shops buying various seeds to plant in our yard. We all know how it works. Dig, fertilize, till, arrange, and drop the seed in the right spot and water. Then just wait and see what happens. At the appointed time, out it pops, and before long another beautiful color is displayed for everyone to see and another sweet fragrance fills the air. You can imagine the shock and surprise when we came home one day in April to find a sign in our front yard that read: "Yard of the Month." "I like that," I thought out loud, convinced I would find a sermon illustration or two to accompany this truly magnificent award.

Have you ever thought about your life being a blessing to God, that you can praise God through your life? Have you ever thought that the way you live can either be pleasing to God or be a source of sadness to Him? Often, we live in a way that our lives are a burden to God: complaining, arguing, disobeying, and ignoring His Word and His will. Here, God is looking at us and saying, "If you want to bless Me, if you want to please Me, you will continually offer up a sacrifice of praise. Your lips will confess Me to others. Your praise will be a blessing to Me." Hebrews 13:16 continues, *Do not forget to do good and to share with others, for with such sacrifices God is pleased.* So by praising God and confessing His name we will be a blessing to Him. Furthermore, the Scriptures teach that by doing good and being kind to others, we will please Him. These don't sound like very hard or challenging things to do—praising God and doing good to others. But I tell you the author would not have had to remind us of these things if we weren't vulnerable to them. The reason why he felt it was necessary to remind us is because we so easily lapse into a state of unconsciousness when it comes to praising God. Some cite business, some blame others, and some simply become neglectful. Whatever our excuses may be, we have to train ourselves to step back and remember why we were put on this earth. It's not for our families, though they are a wonderful blessing from God; it's not for our careers, though they are so essential to our lives. The list could go on and on. The reason God placed us on this earth was to have fellowship with Him through praise and worship.

So far we have mentioned some of the things we *should* do; now, let's examine how we should go about putting these same things into action. We know we can be a blessing to God by offering a sacrifice of praise to Him, and we know that we can be a blessing to God by doing good to others. But how do we put this into practice? Here are six ways we can be a blessing to both God and to others:

1. We can be a blessing to others because we have personal peace.

Have you ever known someone who was not at peace with God or with themselves? It is unpleasant to be around them. They are constantly questioning and second-guessing themselves. They are living a life full of discontent. When a person struggles with life and has no peace, it is impossible to be a blessing to others. Often I meet people who are struggling with this.

One pastor's wife grew up in a home surrounded by great conflict. Her mother had been abused as a child and had a terrible family life. As a result, her mother had carried the generational sin into her marriage and into her home. As this pastor's wife grew up, she had no peace. She accepted Christ into her heart and life but did not realize He could give her peace. Consequently, she was not a blessing to her husband, her children, her church, or her God. Well into her thirties, this woman came to understand that God not only forgives, but He can heal her hurts, too. He certainly could give *her* the ability to forgive others for what they had done to her, but He also would give her the ability to forgive herself. He could give her the kind of personal peace she had never experienced before. This lady became totally transformed as a result. First, she confessed her sin and disobedience to the Lord. Then she accepted God's forgiveness by faith through His Word. Having been forgiven, she entrusted herself to our Savior and began to forgive herself because Christ had forgiven her. Now she was ready to claim Paul's admonition to "be anxious for nothing." Through prayer she made her requests known to God and received the peace of God which passes all human understanding. Now she was ready to start blessing others because she, herself, was set free. Once she realized this important precept and put it into action, she began to minister to others and became a blessing to those around her. She could be a blessing because she had accepted God's life-changing peace.

2. We can be a blessing to others because we have the Great Shepherd.

Throughout the Scriptures, Jesus is referred to as the Great Shepherd. Why is this, do you suppose? Well, a shepherd cares for his sheep. He feeds them, leads them, and watches over them. In John 10:11, Jesus states, *"I am the good shepherd. The good shepherd lays down his life for the sheep."* A shepherd is there to lead, guide, and direct the sheep, to keep them safe from wolves and outside attacks. Shepherds keep watch over their sheep. When just one sheep wanders off, the shepherd is always there to lead him back to safety. But let's face it, folks, sheep are not the smartest of creatures. They need herding; they need guidance. They have to be constantly watched because sheep have a tendency to wander away, and they become easily distracted unless they are under a watchful eye.

Just as a shepherd watches over his flock, so does the Great Shepherd who watches over us. We are His sheep and, consequently, are in need of someone to guide, direct, and protect us from harm. Now, you might be saying, "Hey, wait a minute. I think you just called me a sheep. And just a few minutes ago you said sheep weren't very bright." Yes, I did. You are keeping up nicely. *We* (that is all of us) are just like sheep. Sometimes we aren't very bright. We need a shepherd; we need a guide. When we are fed by His Word, when we are guided by His will, and when we have the comfort of knowing that He is watching over us, it will be easy to be a blessing to others.

3. We can be a blessing to others because we are equipped.

God has given us the ability to be a blessing to others. He has equipped us with gifts, talents, and individualized personalities so that we can be a blessing to Him and to others. In 1 Corinthians 12, Paul discusses the importance of spiritual gifts. In verses 4–6, he writes, *"There are different kinds of gifts, but the same Spirit. There are different kinds of service, but the same Lord. There are different kinds of working, but the same God works all of them in all men."* God has given us spiritual gifts to utilize so we can be a blessing to Him and to others. If you don't know what your gifts are, I urge you to study hard and find out so God can use you to further His Kingdom. One of the many ways I teach our people to discover their giftedness is to ask two very simple questions: "What do I love to do? What gives me great joy?" I have always believed the Lord Jesus gives us the privilege of doing the things we love to do. Think about this for a moment. Do you really believe the Lord goes around saying, "Let Me think of something to give My son or daughter to do. In fact, let's make this as unpleasant as possible. Perhaps I could really teach him a lesson through his service to Me. Anyone who comes after Me and devotes his life to me as a true disciple, will be sentenced to a life of pain, misery, and hardship because I am going to see to it they hate every minute of life and service to their King"? Sounds like God, huh? Really, folks, God will fulfill the desires of your heart. When you ask this question, you will find yourself being drawn into the very area where God can use you to the greatest effect. Do you enjoy little children? Then think about devoting your service to little children. What about teenagers? Do we need you or what? So you don't like to speak in public? How about driving a bus, or helping with the massive area of maintenance and grounds, or helping to organize or harness prayer requests, or fetch and carry senior adults to and from a retirement center. Any question on this matter?

We all know that being equipped for a job is important. If you don't have the right stuff, things aren't going to go well. Can you imagine going on a backpacking trip and forgetting to pack food or water or a compass? Or how about that long-awaited golfing trip with your buddies and you forget to bring your nine-iron and your pitching wedge? Can somebody say "mulligan"? When a baby is born, parents begin equipping the baby from day one. They teach him how to eat, sit up, walk, get dressed, to get along with others, and thousands of other things. We do this because we love our children. As parents, we know that it's our job to equip our children so they can grow, develop and mature into successful adults. God does the same for us by equipping us for the journey of life. He never allows us to run this race without giving us the proper attire and the best equipment. He promises throughout the Scriptures that He has a plan for us, a Kingdom Plan. He has a purpose for each and every one of our lives. He will equip us to do great things. When you have the right skills and the right equipment to do a job, you are confident that you will successfully complete the task. When you are confident that God has given you the skills and equipment to minister to others, you will surely be blessed!

4. We can be a blessing to others because we are being taught.

I don't know about you, but God teaches me something new every day (whether I want to learn or not). There are some days when I don't think I have another thing to learn because I know it all, and those are the days God *really* teaches me a thing or two. No matter what the lesson—strength, hope, perseverance, patience, or love—God is always waiting to reveal a different part of Himself to us. He wants us to know more, to understand more, and to be more. Henry Blackaby has a phenomenal Bible study called *Experiencing God.* One of the main themes in this study is that you have to go where God is in order to experience Him. You can't wait around and expect God to do all the work, make a nice even path for you, and then wait for you. You have to be willing to be taught, to work a little in order to really see God in action. God is not going to push Himself on anyone. Therefore, we have to put our shoulder to the plow and work for it. Some years ago, I had the privilege of preaching in Interlaken, Switzerland, for the European Convention of Baptists. Henry Blackaby taught the Bible studies. What a time it was indeed as dedicated Christian people assembled from all over the European continent. I asked Henry about *Experiencing God* because my entire church had recently undertaken the study together. The Lord had radically spoken to our hearts and as a result had altered the direction of our entire church. His answer was simple, "It's about God, Don!" That's it! And when we are about God, He speaks. He teaches us.

5. We can be a blessing to others because godly people surround us.

One of the greatest joys of being part of the family of God lies in the fact that you and I are surrounded by godly people. They are everywhere. No matter where you go in the world, you will find godly people. That's the church, folks. Most certainly we are blessed with beautiful sanctuaries and paved parking lots. But there is so much more to the family of God. It's not just a sanctuary or a pulpit—it's the people. And it's a wonderful place to be. Being surrounded by godly people will always prove one of the greatest blessings of life because our Savior will use them to be a wonderful source of counsel and blessing. Besides, I need to be kept on the straight and narrow. I need help when I am down. I need to know how to love my wife in a manner which will be pleasing to the Lord. I need help in the rearing of my children. I need godly direction for every turn in the race of life. When a Christian brother puts his hand on my shoulder and gives me godly counsel, I know I'm in a good place. I love the prayers godly people pray for me. I love the support, the encouragement, and the work that godly people do. And do you see what happens here, folks? When I have these kinds of feelings for my brothers and sisters in Christ, I cannot help but be a blessing to them because they are a blessing to me. I believe God smiles on this and He is pleased. I would counsel you to prioritize this critical matter so that you can finish well and strong. Surround yourselves with godly people so you can learn from them, grow with them, and be a blessing to them. And, as you reach for the finish line, make this an un-apologetic mandate for your life.

Let me share something personal with you. One of the wonderful blessings of staying the course and sticking to the task, serving the Lord Jesus in the same place, with the same people, in the same community, is the matter of earned respect. Any leader, no matter what position is occupied, will never function as a leader in the truest sense of the word simply by virtue of the position given. Position given is nothing more than an invitation to acquire position earned. Leadership that leads by virtue of position earned carries with it a far greater level of success than leadership that leads by virtue of position given. I was called and af-firmed by thousands of people to my position given. The day I arrived on the job, I sat in the seat of leadership. But it has taken many years of joy, trial, and tribulation to occupy the seat of position earned. And I believe a key component to the attainment of this wonderful seat on the counsel of elders comes by means of godly access. There are two types of leaders in the work of the Lord. There are those who lead with great personal leadership ability from the seat of their own understanding. And there are those who lead with great leadership ability from the seat of their own understanding in concert with the wisdom of godly counsel and leadership. The former can achieve great things but also can crash and burn while leaving a trail of disillusioned staff and disenfranchised members. The "ownership principle" which is so essential to church growth is all but declared null and void. But the real damage done follows a leader of this nature and leaves his successor to pick up the pieces. The leader who submits to godly leadership and serves together with others will find, with the passing of time, a natural propensity to trust his leadership completely. And the more respect for leadership rises to greater and greater heights, the more imperative it is for the respected leader to defer to the opinions and advice of the same godly council that defers everything to his leadership. And so the cycle of joy begins to turn, fanning into flame all the potential of God's grace brought to bear on those who determine to run the race of life well and finish strong.

6. We can be a blessing to others because we have God's grace.

Grace is God's unmerited favor. This is a central, integral component of Christian living. If you are a believer, then you know that salvation only comes through Jesus Christ. God's grace covers me, and it covers my sins even though I do not deserve it. I did nothing to earn it, I can do nothing to keep it, and I can do nothing to lose it. His grace is sufficient for me.

God's love for us is so vast and so overwhelming that He doesn't stop there. His grace not only allows us to have a relationship with Him, but it also allows us to have countless blessings. My home, my family, the car I drive, the friends I have, my church, my country, everything I have, everything that I am comes out of God's grace. He has blessed me with an abundant life, and not just here and now but an abundant life after I leave this place, too. We can please God by sharing this good news with others, praising Him by confessing His name.

Hebrews 13:15 is clear in its direction. The writer comes right out and says:

- Offer a sacrifice of praise
- Remember to do good
- Share with others

It's so straightforward and simple. Praise your Maker. Develop a relationship of praise with Him. Confess Him to others by letting His name be the fruit of your lips. Do not forget to do what is good and right in the sight of the Lord. The Bible is your guide, and the Holy Spirit will lead you. If you're attuned to God's voice, you will always know the good you ought to do. Share your blessings, gifts and talents with others—love them. And by doing so, you will be obeying the second greatest commandment, "Love one another."

These words are straight down the line. "Okay, people, here's what you do—1, 2, 3." It seems a little odd that the writer tells us things we should already know: praise God, do good to your fellow man, and share all you have with those around you. But because we are fallible, forgetful, and come from a sinful nature, we must be reminded, encouraged to push on. There is a serious recognition here that the race of life we are running is at the *best* of times hard and difficult. As such we have to be cheered on and told again about those things we know to be true in order to make it to the finish line. Even though the race can get tough, we are encouraged never to give up. We have to keep on running; we have to keep on pushing toward that prize which God has called us heavenward in Christ Jesus.

THE ELEVENTH CHAPTER

The Strength of Submission

"True strength lies in submission which permits one to dedicate his life, through devotion, to something beyond himself."

—*Henry Miller*

Scripture Reference: Hebrews 13:17
Obey your leaders and submit to their authority.
They keep watch over you as men who must give an account.
Obey them so that their work will be a joy, not a burden,
for that would be of no advantage to you.

If you want to get people riled up in a hurry, just utter the word "submission" and watch what happens: eyebrows will raise, heads will turn, and mouths will gasp for air. You would think we were talking about murder or hippos stampeding through a busy playground. You know—something really appalling. But, nope, we are talking about submission—a word that is very taboo in our society today. A possible reason for this may well be the fact that the underlying theme of our culture is self: it's doing what I want to do when I want to do it. Such self-centeredness is paradoxical to God's Word. Most people seriously question the need to submit to something greater than ourselves.

Now, I do not single out any principle in God's Word as being more important than any other because all of God's Word is equally significant. However, when God talks to Christians about being submissive, He touches people at a very deep part of their being. Any mention of submissiveness touches the nerve center of the human spirit because few people want to be owned by or subservient to any other person. Christians, in particular, have to deal with this matter because of the inherent nature of the gospel message. There are, perhaps, two reasons why submission has become such a lightening rod to so many, even in the church of God. They are an arrogant attitude and an incorrect perspective. Quite frankly, many of us have a superior attitude that is the result of an arrogant attitude. Perhaps this is a consequence of our sinful human nature. Arrogance was the root cause of the fall of Satan from the presence of God when he determined he wanted to be God. Arrogance expressed itself in Satan's refusal to submit to One who is above all. The serpent in the Garden of Eden convinced Eve to eat of the forbidden fruit. Once again, this exposes the arrogance of the human heart and a refusal to submit to the dictates of the One who is above all. Arrogance exposes the fact we are all sinners by nature and sinners by choice. We say things like, "I know what I am doing—just leave me alone" or "I can make my own decisions. No one can tell me what to do." We have a high view of ourselves, so it is hard for us to listen to someone else. We think we have all the answers. This concept of self invades our way of thinking. We become so swept up by how great we are that we actually begin to believe we don't need to listen to authority. "Oh, that rule is put in place for *them*, not me. I can bend this one rule a little bit and it won't make any difference." An arrogant attitude, consequently, keeps us from being submissive.

Secondly, most of us have an incorrect perspective of what the word "submissive" really means. The word has come to have such a mangled and distorted connotation because it has been misused. In fact, it has been abused. At one time, newspapers and television talk shows buzzed with the shocking story of a man who headed up a polygamous cult out West. His father had been the undisputed prophet of this group of self-styled polygamists and had passed this heinous notion onto his son. Very soon the notion of superiority and special selectivity on the part of his god left him with the "authority" to order the systematic sexual abuse of young girls and boys as well as the "authority" to force young girls into polygamous marriages while engineering a system that drove the younger boys into the wilderness. These boys became known as the "lost boys." This criminal was listed in the FBI's Ten Most Wanted List and was, at the time of this writing, still a fugitive hiding like an animal somewhere out there.

Abuse, unfortunately, can spread to all members of the family. Sad to say, but many wives have suffered years and years of verbal and sexual abuse from husbands who have "lorded" their masculinity over them. So many, literally, suffer in silence.

Is there any wonder why submission has become such a lightening rod to so many? This is not what God teaches us. Submitting to God is merely listening to what He says with an understanding that God knows more than we do. It's really that simple. It's not about being better or being greater, it's about recognizing our place as it relates to a holy and mighty God. That's it.

Hebrews 13:17 reminds us to be submissive. In this case, we are exhorted to submit to our leaders and to those who hold authority over us. Though this principle is simple in nature, it is profoundly critical because it affects us all the time. Everywhere we go, there is someone in charge, and it might not be us. Scriptures teach that we must submit to God. Furthermore, we must submit to our leaders, those who are over us in whatever capacity that might be. We must show respect to those leaders because that is what God wants us to do—period. We submit to others because we are following God's command. Therefore, we are submitting to God.

So, I ask you, "Who are our leaders?" To be honest, it all begins in the home. Boys and girls, young people, your spiritual leaders are your moms and dads. You show me a teenager who is not submissive to God's order in the home, and I will show you a home where the joy is gone. I will show you a home that has a burden placed upon it, and I will show you a home where the disobedient child loses. Hebrews puts this in the right perspective by stating, *It will be of no advantage to you.* Now, let's take it one step further. Mothers and fathers are the spiritual leaders in the home, but God has given the husband the ultimate responsibility to be the head of the family. Ephesians 5:21–25 reads:

> *Submit to one another out of reverence for Christ. Wives, submit to your husbands as to the Lord. For the husband is the head of the wife as Christ is the head of the church, his body, of which he is the Savior. Now as the church submits to Christ, so also wives should submit to their husbands in everything. Husbands, love your wives, just as Christ loved the church and gave himself up for her.*

Ephesians 6:1-4 says:

> *"Children, obey your parents in the Lord, for this is right. 'Honor your father and mother'—which is the first commandment with a promise—'that it may go well with you and that you may enjoy long life on the earth.' Fathers, do not exasperate your children; instead, bring them up in the training and instruction of the Lord."*

The marriage relationship is a picture of Jesus Christ and His bride, which is the church. When parents come to me with problems in their home, problems in their marriage, and problems with their children, many times it's because there is no mutual submission in the family. When the order of authority is distorted, there will be no joy in the home.

Men, it is time to stand up and become the spiritual leaders in your home. Love your wives as Christ loves the church. Submit to the Lord, and make decisions that are the very best for your wife and children. Do not discourage or frustrate your children, but bring them up in the training and instruction of the Lord. The earliest concept children have of God is greatly influenced by the relationship they have with their fathers. Teach them how to love and how to make wise decisions. Model wise behavior in front of them; get involved and listen to them. Be careful not to dampen their spirits.

Wives, submit to your husbands as unto the Lord. Do you allow your husband to be the head of your home? Many times it is difficult for a man to "wear the pants" in the family because his wife already has them on! Ladies, submission is not an inferior position. Just ask my wife. She is respected; she is admired; she is cherished in our home. She gladly takes this role because I, in turn, make every effort to do what God has commanded me to do—I love her. Now, do I fail? You bet! More times than I could ever count. She, in turn, responds to me in love. Karyn and I believe we are equal partners in everything we do. As we discussed in a previous chapter, I am the man, she is the woman. And our primary responsibility toward one another is to spend a lifetime making it possible for each to be the absolute best man and best woman, the most fulfilled man and the most fulfilled woman, in the whole wide world. Believe it or not, this involves mutual submission. Whether it is a wife to her husband, a husband to his wife, or a child to his parent, both men and women are created equal. We just have different functions in the family. If we all ran around doing the same thing, something would be left out, forgotten. This is why God has given order to the family structure, so that everything will fall into place and be well looked after.

Submission to one another also breeds respect in children. One mother came to her pastor brokenhearted over her son's response to her husband. Earlier that morning, her son and husband had a confrontation over the son's rebellious behavior. The son stood up in his father's face and blurted out, "Don't tell me what to do. You're stupid!" The pastor, knowing the strained relationship between the mother and father, asked the mother, "Where do you think your son got the idea that his father is stupid? And why did your son think it was in some way acceptable for him to utter such words against his father?" The mother dropped her head and replied, "I suppose he learned that from me because I tend to bring up my husband's faults in front of the children. Oh, what have I done?" This mother's actions and her choice of words upset the order of her home. She was not respecting her husband; she was using words unbecoming of a Christian, so she inadvertently soiled her son's perspective of his father. We have all been there, haven't we? All of us say things we regret. All of us blow a fuse. All of us fire back when cornered. All of us justify our actions by blaming the actions of others. But two wrongs never make a right. Parents, watch what you say. Your children are always listening.

Stand together as the spiritual leaders in your home, and do not create an atmosphere in which your children will be invited to play you against one another. Agree in private how to discipline and train your children, then stand firm; keep a united front when dealing with them. Don't contradict one another's discipline. Mothers and fathers will give an account as to how they keep watch over their families. When families submit to one another out of respect for Christ, there will be great joy in the home.

Spiritual leadership starts in the home and flows into the church. And few of us would have any great difficulty in identifying such spiritual leaders. Among others, they include Sunday school teachers, discipleship leaders, Bible study leaders, ministry team members, church deacons, and elders—whatever form of government you might have in your church. God has put leaders there for a reason.

It does not take much to figure out that the Evangelical Church in America is in a state of crisis. Churches of every denomination are closing their doors left and right because they are experiencing great internal conflict. It seems we hear constantly about churches that have become battlegrounds. Have you ever heard of churches where business meetings are war zones? The blueprint is all too much the same. Very often, certain men and women show up at these "business" meetings with a few chosen "allies" in tow. Some of these people have not actually been in worship services in a long time but are still on the membership rolls. The leader of the pack made phone calls and gossip abounds. In many cases, it does not take long for the "chosen" leader to stand and begin his point of opposition by reminding all those assembled just how much "he loves his church" and just how important it is for him to "protect" the church from any and all forms of harm and danger. With all the respect of my heart, I came to believe that these people are the true "blood clots" in the local church. They need to be identified and dealt with from a biblical perspective in a timely and decisive manner. It will prevent the church from suffering a heart attack, which could leave the body weak and ineffective or even dead! But this is the subject of another book. Suffice it to say, the root problem here revolves around the subject of submission or a lack thereof. There are men and women who stand up in churches and say, "Unless I know about it, unless it runs through me, then I don't approve of it because I, quite frankly, don't trust them to make a good decision." This kind of behavior is not acceptable in the church and cannot be pleasing to the Lord Jesus.

When I was eighteen years old, I was an officer in the South African army. We had no choice in those days. All able-bodied young men were conscripted into the armed forces straight out of high school and were forced to defend a system of government few of us supported. On one occasion during my service time, I learned a valuable lesson that later spared me some potential major injury. Our entire company was on parade when a noncommissioned officer came marching by. He did not like me very much, and his disdain for me caused him to commit the ultimate crime: he did not salute me. My rank dictated that he do that; my position demanded it! My whole company saw what happened. Because of my position, I had the power to make his life miserable, even to the point of court-martial.

One of the men in my company approached me and said, "Just let me know when you want to proceed with action against him." I looked him squarely in the eye and said, "I do not plan to take action against him." I could hear the rumble of murmurs run through the ranks of men because few of them had much respect for this man either. "But Lieutenant, he didn't salute you! With all due respect, sir, you have every right to court-martial him." I replied solemnly, "Yes, I know I have every right to throw him in the brig, but I have no intention of doing that. You see, I would much prefer he salute me not because of my position but because he respects me." Three months later, that very man saved my life in a very difficult situation in the desert of Southwest Africa, now known as Namibia. He became my biggest supporter and friend. The same principle holds true with the church. We must have mutual submission and respect for one another in order for the church to be what God intended for it to be.

The church is the body of Christ, not a building made up of green carpet and beige paint. So, how does the body of Christ function? The Bible tells us that some of us are the hands, some of us are the feet, and some of us are the eyes, but only Christ is the head of the church. As the body of Christ, we are enabled to function, and ultimately thrive, as long as we work in unison. Mutual submission among all believers within the church is necessary to carry out the work God has given us to do. Otherwise, it does not work smoothly. Malfunctions are bound to occur, and significant meltdowns and even blowups of a very serious nature can surface. If one part of the body does not submit, the whole body does not function properly. If your back is broken, you're not going anywhere. If your hand is on strike, if your arm throws in the towel, or if your leg decides to call it quits, guess what? You're in big trouble, my friend.

You show me a business where people do not submit to each other, and I will show you chaos. You show me a basketball team where one member thinks he's God's special gift to the team, and I'll show you a mediocre team. Remember the great Los Angeles Lakers' team that went to the NBA finals and lost? How could this be with Kobe and Shaq and a host of the best players in the NBA? I was not there, neither am I much of a basketball expert, but the news reporters certainly spoke of the lack of unity on the team. This was just a nice way to point out the lack of submission between men of such exceptional ability. The same, perhaps, is true of the United States Ryder Cup team. How is it possible to have golfers like Phil Mickelson, Tiger Woods, Chris Di-Marco, Jim Furyk, and Davis Love playing "together" and still lose to a European team of greats but not "giants" in my humble but very accurate opinion? Submission to one another is not degrading; it does not dismiss our unique gifts. True submission, when utilized correctly, highlights *all* the gifts of the individuals involved. It brings us together; it displays the power of working together.

Let me use "Building Together in Faith" as an illustration. Several years ago, our church commissioned a group of people to examine the needs for additional space because our church had grown significantly. We wanted to provide adequate space for people, especially for our children and youth, for the future. This group was given the task of bringing a recommendation to the deacons regarding the future building plans for our church. After months of meeting together, they brought a recommendation to the deacons. They discussed the recommendation to great lengths, submitted to one another, and brought it to the church family. I will never forget that Wednesday night meeting; it was so overwhelmingly positive. And so we embarked on this incredible project, Building Together in Faith. I want to single out one man here, Mr. Carroll Cox. He had just retired as an engineer with Lockwood Greene. He is a highly esteemed member of our church. I love him with all of my heart. God led this man to be there morning, noon, and night. He, along with countless others, devoted time and effort to manage what God led us to do. During that entire process, I never told him what to do, or demanded to know what was going on. Why? Because I trusted him and submitted to his authority as the leader God had chosen for that project. You cannot micromanage the ministry of God's work.

Another example is the finance team of a church. You elect a wonderful group of people to be on the finance team. These men and women can be trusted. They know about finances. Let them do their work. Bring in someone to do an independent audit every year and ensure a sound system of checks and balances. But let those designated to do the work do their work. When the finance team brings a recommendation to the church, trust that they have done their job. The day any person stands up in a church and says, "I will not vote for that until I have seen it for myself," is the day we stand in the face of God, and say, "I will not submit to the body of Christ." With that kind of attitude, we will never accomplish the work God has called us to do.

Suppose I went to the minister of music in our church and said, "Steve, I know God has called you to be the minister of music in this church, but I am the senior pastor. I have been given charge of everything, from Genesis to Revelation. It's all mine! Steve, I just want you to know that as of tomorrow, every song, every worship service you plan—I need to approve it. If I do not see the song beforehand, we are not singing it." Ha! We would be in trouble because we would sing "Jingle Bells" every Sunday (my knowledge of music is about as deep as a kiddie pool). This is precisely why God has given us all different gifts. We must submit to one another's leadership and authority.

Let's look at Hebrews 13:7 again: *Obey your leaders and submit to their authority. They keep watch over you as men who must give an account. Obey them so that their work will be a joy.* When you do not submit to one another in the church, you rob your leaders of their joy. When you do not submit to one another in your home, you rob yourself of joy. Nobody wins!

The next part of the verse reads, "Not a burden, for that would be of no advantage to you." Are you one of those people who becomes a

burden to others in your church by standing up in a business meeting
and proclaiming, "I want you to know, I don't care how much work has
been done on this project, I won't accept it until I see it for myself"? Excuse me—not in the house of God. You may have the idea that you
know everything about everything, but the Bible says that kind of an attitude will be of no advantage to you. At this point, you may be thinking, "Pastor, what does all of this mean? I hear what you're saying, but
how can I put this into practice?" Let me suggest five principles of submissiveness which may be a blessing to you:

Principle #1: Trust

When I submit to other Christians, I am saying, "God, I can trust you."
Recently, our deacons chose a group of men to make a recommendation.
This sub-group did their work and reported back to the larger body.
Many wonderful questions were asked and many answers were given.
The final analysis, the bottom line—they came out with an unbelievable
recommendation to the church with the entire group standing together
as one man. Herein lies the essence of mutual submission. It's not si-
lence; it is not in any way denigrating individual giftedness. It's the cul-
mination of wonderful gifts working together to bring about the will of
God. It is trust in its truest form.

Principle #2: Acknowledge

What does it mean to be submissive? It means you are acknowledging
the work of the Spirit in other people; you are acknowledging God. A
man who doesn't acknowledge the work of God in others is certainly
not willing to be submissive to God. He says, (whether it is out loud or
by his actions) "Are you kidding me? The Spirit only speaks through
me. I know best." I think we all know better than this. God's Spirit
dwells in all people who know and love Jesus Christ. If we're not will-

ing to be submissive to others, how can we ever get the job done? In a church organization such as ours, the issue of the acknowledgement of individual giftedness has a practical application of major significance. Many organizations operate on "the imperative to call a meeting" principle. This compulsion is based on the "membership" principle by which virtue the "ownership" principle operates. Everybody owns, therefore everybody must always decide. Very little can be accomplished doing things like this. Hence the imperative to let committees do all the work of the church. Committees or teams, as we call them, are small groups of gifted people who do the work related to their area or assignment. And, please note, there is a huge difference between committees that do the work of the church and committees that run the church. I would never want to serve a church run by committees.

Principle #3: Value

This third principle is so important as we strive to run the race of life and finish well. It begs the question be asked yet again. What does it mean to be submissive? It means we value the work of other people. When I submit to someone who is a spiritual leader, I value what that person does. Much of the problem in the evangelical church today is there are too many people who do not value one another. We are like the show *Crossfire*—we don't listen to what other people are saying, and we are too concerned with getting our own point across. For the church to grow and be vibrant, it has to stand on the principles of God; we have to respect one another by being submissive. We must value what other people do.

When you value what other people do, you will not be critical of them. Often, it's easy to go home on Sunday and have "fried pastor" or "fried youth pastor" for lunch. Besides, this constant criticism of leaders is risky in front of the children. When you are critical of your pastor, youth pastor, or other church leaders in the presence of your children, sooner or later they will lose respect for them. Such demonstrable behavior can be so detrimental to the child and his future. It is amazing to watch some of these behaviors being passed from one generation to the next. When respect is lost, a lack of submission will be a result. Value what others do. A critical spirit will have no advantage for you or your family.

Principle #4: Admit

One of the most difficult things to do for most people is to admit faults and weaknesses. Admitting something is simply owning up to the fact that whatever is needed to be done cannot be accomplished without help. Therein lies the essence of submission again. If you want to be submissive, you must admit there is too much work to be done by yourself. If you want to be submissive, you have to allow others the chance to prove their giftedness. I happen to be the senior pastor of my church, and a major part of my assignment is to provide overall spiritual leadership. But not even the archangel Gabriel can do it all. Not on your life, absolutely not. We have many godly people in the church who are very competent and willing to serve. They are just as capable and, in many cases, far more accomplished. Ironically, we hurt ourselves and everyone else when we fail to admit we need help from others. We must submit to one another and accept the fact that there is too much work to be done for just one person.

Besides all of this, there is too much to do. There are lives to be saved. God's work to be done. It is so sad to hear individuals speak as though they have been specially selected by God to be the only mouthpiece of His wisdom. I know some may think, "I would never say that to anyone." But that is precisely what is said when the work and giftedness of others is questioned by those who see themselves as "God's special gift to mankind." Please realize that time is fleeting. We have too much work to do.

Principle #5: Volunteer

Volunteerism is the heartbeat of America. So much good is accomplished as a result in nearly every sector of life. Volunteerism is the practical component of submission. It is applied submissiveness. Sadly, many remain seated rather than standing up and being counted. If we are not submissive, if we do not offer our abilities in submission to God, then we are denying His Word. Think about all the combined giftedness it takes to produce the sound that flows from an orchestra. Although I would love to do so, I have never conducted an orchestra. In fact, I do not know a flute from a piccolo, but I do know how beautiful it sounds when every instrument is playing in sync with every other instrument. Can you imagine if the drummer decided he wanted to show off and began banging his drum as loud as he could? Or what about the trumpet player—what if he wanted to "toot his own horn" quite literally? This would ruin the sweet sound of teamwork exemplified in an orchestra. When Christians submit to the authority of their spiritual leaders and every person in their own giftedness bears their part in the body of Christ, there will be a sweet harmony that rises up out of the church. But each instrument has to be present for the combined sound of music to be heard. Perhaps this is why it is so important to volunteer. Your place is reserved for you, and you are needed no matter how small the part or position.

In a society where people confuse submission with inferiority, it's easy to see why there is such debate on this subject. I believe if submission was better understood, there would be so much less controversy over the matter. People would gladly accept their roles; the hands do this, the feet do that, and the eyes do the other. We would rely on the giftedness of others to make the *whole* body function the way God intended it to function. Whether this takes place in the home or at church, we would revel in our strengths and entrust others where we are weak. There is great vulnerability in submission. God has ordered that we each have a distinct function, that we all have a role in our families and in our churches. Perhaps a fresh understanding will help to run the race of life well and finish strong. The Word of God must always have the last word. As we consider these things, take a fresh look at Paul's instruction to the new church in Corinth. Writing in 1 Corinthians 12:12–26, he says:

> *The body is a unit, though it is made up of many parts; and though all its parts are many, they form one body. So it is with Christ. For we were all baptized by one Spirit into one body— whether Jews or Greeks, slave or free—and we were all given the one Spirit to drink. Now the body is not made up of one part but of many. If the foot should say, "Because I am not a hand, I do not belong to the body," it would not for that reason cease to be part of the body. And if the ear should say, "Because I am not an eye, I do not belong to the body," it would not for that reason cease to be part of the body. If the whole body were an eye, where would the sense of hearing be? If the whole body were an ear, where would the sense of smell be? But in fact God has arranged the parts in the body, every one of them, just as he wanted them to be. If they were all one part, where would the body be? As it is, there are many parts, but one body. The eye cannot say to the hand, "I don't need you!" And the head cannot say to the feet, "I don't need you!" On the contrary, those parts of the body that seem to be weaker are indispensable, and the parts that we think are less honorable we treat with special honor. And the parts that are unpresentable are treated with special modesty, while our presentable parts need no special treatment. But God has combined the members of the body and has given greater honor to the parts that lacked it, so that there should be no division in the body, but that its parts should have equal concern for each other. If one part suffers, every part suffers with it; if one part is honored, every part rejoices with it.*

There it is in a nutshell. One body with many parts all working in union with each other. There is no jostling for position here. There are no egos out there, just mutual submission. What a glorious way to run the race of life.

THE TWELFTH CHAPTER

The Potential of Prayer

*"To be a Christian without prayer is no more possible
than to be alive without breathing."*

—*Martin Luther King, Jr.*

Scripture Reference: Hebrews 13:18–19 (NLT)
*Pray for us, for our conscience is clear and we want to live honorably
in everything we do. I especially need your prayers right now
so that I can come back to you soon.*

It's confession time in the race of life! The single greatest weakness most of us have in our personal and corporate lives is prayer. We need to come clean and confess this to the Lord. Most powerful and effective men and women who have lived lives of great influence and value point to prayer as the key. The writer to the Hebrews makes a staggering announcement himself when he claims a "clear conscience" and a desire "to live honorably in everything we do." How desperately we need to be able to come to the end of our lives with such statements of fact at hand. I want a clear conscience, and I most certainly desire to live honorably in everything I do. The question is, how to do this? The key is prayer, and our Savior made this point emphatically.

"Ask and it will be given to you; seek and you will find; knock and the door will be opened to you. For everyone who asks receives; he who seeks finds; and to him who knocks, the door will be opened" (Matthew 7:7–8).

Have you ever considered the full potential of prayer? Have you thought about what the power of prayer can do? There is an awesome exchange that occurs when we pray. It's amazing, absolutely remarkable! When we lift our prayers to God, whether we are in our cars, at our dining room tables, in our pews, or at our desks, we are having a conversation with the all-powerful, all-knowing God, the Maker of the universe. He has the power to change lives and to bring healing. He has the power to convict and forgive. The power of prayer is astounding, and the potential it carries is phenomenal. The authority of God is behind it, therefore, *"If you believe, you will receive whatever you ask for in prayer"* (Matthew 21:22).

As Christians, we not only need to love one another and submit to one another, but we need to pray for one another. The race set before us is challenging at the best of times. There are mountains and valleys, rough terrain, and rolling hills we must traverse. We all face hard times, sad times, victories, and struggles. No matter what the circumstances, though, whether we are on top of a mountain or in a deep, dark valley, we need prayer. Intercession from others will allow us to make it through and stay strong. Praying for others will help them keep running the race so they, too, can finish strong.

In Hebrews 13:18, the writer is in essence saying, "We need prayer. Our task is hard, and we need supernatural help." Two things strike me here about the author's word.

First, he knows how difficult the road can be, how taxing the race is on both the mind and the body. Second, he is humble enough to say, "I need you. I can't do this alone. Please pray for me." These are key components to prayer. In the former, the writer sets the example for us by admitting it's tough out there. A clear conscience and pure spirit are necessities in doing God's work, but they are so hard to maintain. It takes great effort and much prayer to keep a heart clean and uncontaminated from the temptations of this world. In the latter, he sets the example for us by demonstrating a humble and vulnerable spirit. He asks for prayer; he shares his burdens. I think often in our *churches* today, we do not share our struggles openly. I think often in our *homes* today, we do not share our burdens freely. Sadly, these are two places where we should feel the most comfortable in letting our struggles be known.

As evidenced in Hebrews, the author knows the potential of prayer. He understands that it is critical in maintaining a clear conscience and an honorable life. He realizes that in order for God to work through him, he must have others praying on his behalf. Most people have experienced the power of prayer. Often, we spend time in our churches praying for the sick, those who have immediate physical needs, but how often do we pray for others to have a clear conscience? How often do we pray for others to live honorably? When's the last time you asked someone to lift you up in prayer because you were struggling with your conscience? I think we fail to do this because it is easier to voice a physical ailment than a spiritual one; it's easier to pray for a broken leg or an impending surgery than it is to pray for more intimate matters. No one wants to say, "Excuse me, I've been really struggling with my quiet time lately. It just seems like I'm talking to the ceiling." But we will come right out and offer, "Please pray for me. I have a sinus infection." It's seems so much easier to ask for or offer up prayers that cover surface issues only. It takes a certain level of humility and vulnerability to admit we need help, that we need prayer.

It's even harder to pray for the will of God. Selfishly, we pray for things *we* think need to happen and not for God's will in the situation. We pray for things to go this way, or that way, as long as the way is suitable to us. "Thy kingdom come, thy will be done." Ring a bell? In Matthew 6:9–13, Jesus models for us how to pray.

> *"This, then, is how you should pray: 'Our Father in heaven, hallowed be your name, your kingdom come, your will be done on earth as it is in heaven. Give us today our daily bread. Forgive us*

our debts, as we also have forgiven our debtors. And lead us not into temptation, but deliver us from the evil one.'"

In the third Gospel, we see Jesus struggle with this very same concept shortly before His crucifixion. Here we find our Savior on the Mount of Olives praying, not only for His disciples but also for Himself. The Scripture reads, *"He withdrew about a stone's throw beyond them, knelt down and prayed, 'Father, if you are willing, take this cup from me; yet not my will, but yours be done'"* (Luke 22:41–42).

One can hardly imagine the battle taking place between Jesus Christ, who is man, and Jesus Christ, who is God. A closer scrutiny of this dramatic moment will throw some light on the content of His battle. Jesus knows His death is fast approaching. As a human, the impending pain is too much to bear. He cries out in the flesh for deliverance but, as God, He stakes His claim and stands firm by crying, "Not My will, but Yours be done." A truly remarkable moment in time. A moment when the sinfulness of man and the holiness of God met in the garden of Gethsemane. A moment when prayer became the anchor. A moment when a conversation with God produced ultimate triumph and victory. A moment when the line was drawn and the Son of God surrendered to the divine will of the Father, who is in heaven. The moment at which our pardon was set in motion.

And this is how we should pray. Even when we know that God's will requires pain or suffering on our part, maybe even a bit of sacrifice, we still must pray according to the will of God.

The closing remarks in Hebrews 13 pull us back in line. We are reminded that life is not about us. It's not about *our* will, but God's. It's not about running the race in *our* strength, but relying upon God for His sovereign power. There are three specific areas highlighted in this special word from God's Word. Each of these areas opens up vast arenas of expression in and through our own lives. They include the need to pray concerning matters of conscience, conduct, and God's will.

We need to pray concerning the matter of conscience.

The matter of conscience is critical to our understanding of human nature and sin. All human beings have a conscience. In raw terms, a person's conscience is clearly defined as that inner sense of what is right or wrong in one's conduct or motives. And this inner sense moves the individual (hopefully) toward right action. One would hope and pray that all civilized people would follow the dictates of their consciences. Ultimate decisions related to a person's behavior are based on the complex of ethical and moral principles that control or inhibit the actions of the individual. It follows that proper upbringing, mentoring, education, and even cultural heritage all play an important role in the development and expression of a person's actions produced and governed by the conscience. Many of our jails are full because some people evidently have allowed their consciences to be duped into submission. Many a judge has heard the words, "Your Honor, I truly thought the better for doing what I did, but my weak side got hold of me and I acted before I could think properly." In summary, they laid their conscience aside or just simply did not have a strong enough base of a conscience on which to stand and fight.

The Christian conscience referred to here is entirely another matter. This is not about natural goodness, kindness, or even the propensity to make the right decisions based upon the neighborhood or the culture of education. Rather, this points directly to the righteousness of God in Christ Jesus. In this regard, prayer is the connection between the believer and the source from which matters of the conscience can be addressed. The believer acts the way he acts because he is acting according to the dictates of a righteous God. In his first letter, the apostle Peter calls on all Christians to "be holy because God is holy." Prayer is the means by which we "tap" into the One with whom we are connected. The One who is in us. He is our source, and He is our sustenance. God's righteousness is the standard-bearer of the believer's conscience.

The procedure to be followed must begin with confession because the matter of the spiritual conscience is essentially a matter of the heart. Only God's Spirit can convict a person of sin and the subsequent need to confess all sin to the Lord Jesus Christ. In Psalm 139:23, David says, *Search me, O God, and know my heart.* Only God can know the heart of a person. And confession leaves the believer with a pure heart, a pure conscience before God.

A clear conscience will do two things for us. First, it will enable us to be bold in approaching God in prayer. When a child takes cookies from the cookie jar without her parents' knowledge, she will often hide to eat them for fear of being found out. When we are involved in sin, we do the same thing. We don't want to be found out. We want to eat our cookies in secret. Second, a clear conscience will enable us to be bold in ministering to others. If we are involved in sin, it is natural to feel inferior. We look around our Sunday school class and wonder, "Do they know what I did last night? I bet they would never do that." It is vital to have and to keep a clear conscience. Without it, we lack boldness in approaching God and in ministering to others.

We need to pray concerning matters of conduct.

The way we live is far more important than what we say. If the conduct of a spiritual leader is contradictory to their leadership, the entire church will be affected. If we put a drop of red paint into a gallon of pure, white paint, that one little drop would taint the entire thing. If our conduct is unbecoming of a Christian, we taint Christ's name. We need to pray that *our leaders* have godly conduct and a clear conscience. We need to pray that we have godly conduct and a clear conscience. As Christians, we have to be ever cautious that our actions match our beliefs. In matters of godly conduct, we must live a life that is pleasing to God. Prayer will provide that vital link between faith and action. James talks about this at length in his letter. In chapter 1:5, he puts it like this: *"If any of you lacks wisdom, he should ask God, who gives generously to all without finding fault, and it will be given to him."* What a verse! If there is anything we lack in the journey of life, it is the wisdom to conduct ourselves in a manner that is well pleasing to our Savior and Lord. Pray. Ask the Lord to give it to you. He will grant your request.

It is impossible for any person to live a perfect life. We all know this. Even Paul spoke about the war that raged within him. We just can't do it. But we can pray, and we can have others pray for us. We can pray that God will convict us of unpleasing conduct and that He will mold us to ways that are in line with His.

Perhaps we want to consider the order in which God has instructed us in these matters. In simple terms, confession leads to cleansing, which results in godly conduct. In 1 John 1:8, we are reminded that if we are willing to confess our sin to the Lord Jesus Christ, then, because He is a faithful Savior and a just God, He will not only forgive us for all those sins but cleanse us from all our unrighteousness as well. Prayer, once again, is the key component on our part. Through prayer we confess, then we receive forgiveness, then we are declared clean. Christian conduct is the product of a heart in tune with God and right before God. We must pray for one another in regard to these things. Godly conduct will be a natural outcome of a life lived in prayer. Thus, we will be able to finish well. But while the matter of conscience and the matter of conduct are critical, the matter of knowing and doing the will of God is supreme if we are to run the race of life and finish well.

We need to pray concerning matters of God's will.

God called both me and my wife into the ministry many years ago. There we were. Newlyweds, going along happily, and suddenly God interrupted our plans. I remember so clearly the day I knew the Lord was calling me to serve Him for the rest of my life as a full-time vocational preacher and teacher of His Word. I stood up, looked at Karyn, and said, "I believe the Lord is calling me into the ministry!" As I shared earlier in the book, ours was no ordinary calling in that we lived on the other side of the world and God was calling us to come to the United States of America and prepare for our life's work for the Lord Jesus Christ. I had been preparing to study for a Ph.D. at some university overseas, but in all honesty, preferably somewhere in the British commonwealth of nations where cricket was played and having tea still meant stopping for an hour and being served a piping-hot cup of the good old stuff with proper milk in it and a scone covered in jam and clotted cream. But God had a far better plan in mind. He knew, long before we had even the slightest inclination, that our hearts would be inextricably intertwined with our beloved American people in a way we could never have had the slightest hope of grasping back then.

The problem for us, though, was that we both came from very close and loving families. The thought of going to live overseas for who knows how long was not very exciting in terms of those we loved so very much. So how did this all come together? Perhaps something in my story may prove to be a blessing to you in your journey as you make that commitment to know and do the will of God.

We begin with confession of sin. God heard us and cleansed us. Our conscience was now clear in that our minds were positioned to hear from the Lord. The means of making the right decisions were based on a solid foundation. Our conduct was brought in line with the mind of God. Our hearts were now fertile soil ready to receive whatever it was the Lord had to say to us. Then there was the combination of the Word of God and the people of God. Remember how the Lord used J. Roy McComb from Mississippi to bring God's message to me? My life verses, in fact, have become Genesis 12:1-4: *The LORD had said to Abram, 'Leave your country, your people and your father's household and go to the land I will show you.* The bottom line is found in verse 4: *So Abram left as the Lord had told him.*

The final confirmation, so to speak, would come to me through the response of my earthly father. With a tad bit of nervousness, I called my parents and told them the news. My mother was not in the slightest bit surprised God had confirmed His call upon my life. My father listened quietly when I told him we were moving to the United States and then said these words, which have stuck in my heart and soul and have blessed me beyond reason. These are the words I have tried to pass on to my own offspring, and these are the words that hit the nerve of what it means to pray concerning the will of Almighty God. "My son," my dad said, "your mother and I are delighted the Lord Jesus has called you and our precious Karyn into full-time work for Him. I know the United States of America is on the other side of the world. And I know we are going to be separated by thousands of miles. But I want you to know that if your mother and I never see you ever again on this earth, but we know you are in the center of the will of God, our joy will have been made complete." Phew! Wow! Karyn's parents, too, never questioned either our call or the direction God was leading us.

I have often wondered what would have become of me had I not determined to know and do the will of God. I do know that I, too, am only a product of God's grace. Nothing more and nothing less. I often wonder about my children. Today they all love the Lord Jesus Christ. I truly believe it all began for our family when my dad and Karyn's dad laid everything aside to follow the Lord Jesus. Both dads could have continued with their lives with great success, I am sure. But God spoke to them. He called them to forsake their nets. And they did. Both dads have spent a lifetime serving the Lord Jesus alongside our mothers. Today my sons, Rob and Greg, are passionate about Ignite Ministries and about serving the Lord Jesus with all of their hearts. I have often wondered what would have become of me, my wife, my family, and my grandchildren had I not obeyed the Lord's call to serve Him.

We must lift each other up in prayer concerning the will of God. This is so very important. He has a Kingdom Plan for each and every one of us, and we should seek to know what that is. The only way this will happen is by digging into His Word and developing a relationship with Him. If we do this, we will know His will. Consider, for example, my relationship with my wife. Because I have such an open and loving relationship with her and know her so well, I pretty much know what she wants me to do and not do. I know when she wants me to mow the lawn when it starts to grow. She doesn't have to ask me to do that. I know she wants me to take the trash out when it gets full. She doesn't have to write it on a honey-do list for me. I know my wife, therefore I know her will. If I know God and have a deep, abiding relationship with Him, I will know His will.

Being Prayerful Changes Lives.

Let me share a wonderful story with you about the power of prayer. Several years ago, I started receiving critical letters in the mail. Someone went to great lengths to let me know they didn't agree with the way I was conducting myself as the pastor of their church. The letters contained outrageous accusations and language that made my heart very sad. Every letter was on a page that had been torn out of a religious publication. This person would cut and paste letters together to make his point. This went on for months, and each letter seemed to be a little more hostile than the last.

At first, the letters came to the church, and then they began to be delivered to our home. This made the situation even more serious because my children faced the possibility of reading one of them. Karyn and I decided to say nothing and do nothing except pray for this person, whoever it was. One day my wife went to the mailbox and found our usual letter of criticism. This time, however, she called me to tell me. When she started to explain to me what she had received, I was afraid she would be very upset, even frightened. Quite to the contrary—she was laughing! I said, "Karyn, what is so funny?" Through her laughter, she said, "Don, you will not believe what our friend has done. He forgot to take the mailing label off of the magazine before he sent it!" His name was right there on the back page.

Now, I knew who this man was, and I was shocked to think he would do such a thing. He was a long-standing member of the church, a family man, and a deacon. My wife and I prayed for several days for wisdom on how to handle this situation.

Finally, one day I asked him to come to my office for a meeting. When he arrived, I told him that someone had been sending me critical letters, accusing me of ridiculous conduct that was not true. He face began to redden, and his body language was very indignant. He said, "Well, Pastor, what does that have to do with me? Are your accusing me of sending those letters to you?"

I replied very kindly, "Oh, no, I am not accusing you at all. But I do think you need to know that whoever this person is, he has sent the letters on a page torn from a religious publication. The last page he sent had a mailing label affixed to the back of it, and it had *your* name on it. This person *must* have taken *your* magazine. Maybe whoever it is, he is trying to set you up. I asked you to come here today, so we can pray for this person. We need the Lord's direction on how to handle this."

This man was visibly shaken. He stood up and said, "I will find out who is doing this! I will not have someone using my name like that." The letters stopped, and the man was scarce around the church for several months. I continued to pray for him and his precious wife. I prayed for God to convict his heart and to quicken his conscience. I prayed for his conduct and for God's will to be done in the situation.

One day he showed up at my office. His face was soft, and he seemed very different. He said, "Pastor, I just came by to let you know I found out who was sending those letters to you. I have dealt with him, and he has left the church. You will not have to worry about him anymore. I would prefer not to tell you who it was. I would not want you to be disappointed in this man. He is deeply sorry that he caused you this heartache." With that, he turned and left my office. We never mentioned the situation again, and I never received another letter. That man was a faithful and loving member in my church for many years to come. I love him, and to this day I know he loves me.

What if I had allowed emotion to cloud my judgment in that situation? I have to admit there's a part of me that would have felt pretty good in just letting him have it. What if I had confronted him with anger or hostility? I know I could have told him a thing or two after receiving that kind of mail at my home. But, most importantly, what if I had failed to pray for him? I think the situation would have turned out very differently.

As Christians, we must pray for one another. I hope that you are to the point in your walk with the Lord that you understand the depth and the power of prayer; I hope you know the potential prayer carries. We have full and complete access to a holy and just God merely through the utterance of a few words. Yes, our prayers should be filled with humble petitions regarding physical ailments, family problems, and the general well-being of our friends and families. However, as we mature spiritually, our prayers for others should include matters of conscience, of conduct, and of God's will. Being prayerful will not only change the lives of others, but it will also give you the strength and the wisdom to carry out the work God has purposed for you to do. Prayer is the single most fundamental way we have to communicate with our Maker. We must utilize its power and *in everything, by prayer and petition, with thanksgiving, present your requests to God. And the peace of God, which transcends all understanding, will guard our hearts and minds in Jesus Christ* (Philippians 4:6–7). We've got a race to run, folks. We can't run it without breathing; we can't live it without praying.

THE THIRTEENTH CHAPTER

The Race of Faith Finish Line: Final Thoughts

I have fought the good fight, I have finished the race, I have kept the faith.

—2 Timothy 4:7

Scripture Reference: Hebrews 12:1–2 (NKJV)

*Therefore we also, since we are surrounded by so great a cloud of witnesses,
let us lay aside every weight, and the sin which so easily ensnares us, and let us run
with endurance the race that is set before us, looking unto Jesus, the author
and finisher of our faith, who for the joy that was set before Him endured the cross,
despising the shame, and has sat down at the right hand of the throne of God.*

On September 11, 2001, Todd Beamer, along with a group of exceedingly brave people on board United Flight 93, stood up and took action. They knew they were in trouble, they devised a plan, and they carried it out. In speculation, had Flight 93 not crashed into that field in Pennsylvania, where might it have crashed? What might have been the cost? What would have happened if one gentleman had not stood up and said, "Enough talk; we know what we need to do. Let's roll!"

Friends, we don't need to discuss, we don't need to ask for permission, and we don't need to wonder. God's will for us is clear. He has it all written down for us in black and white. It is up to us to read it, understand it, and put it into practice. We've got to take action. We've got to put His words into practice. We know what God expects from us. We know what He would have us do. When we read His Word, He looks into our hearts and says, "It's time to roll. I will lead you. I have already led the way. Be brave and let's go."

You see, friends, He knows the consequences if we stay in our seats; He knows the cost if we decide to do nothing. We've got to get up from the places where we sit and say, "Here I am, Lord. Send me." I urge you to put into practice what you have learned; make today count. I hope this book has inspired you to put on your running shoes. I hope you will get them out of the closet and dust them off because we have a race to run. Friends, we must love like Jesus; realize God has a Kingdom Plan for our lives; walk in others' shoes; love, honor, and cherish our spouses; be content; follow our godly leaders; know the truth; develop a relationship of praise with our Maker; realize the strength we find in submitting to godly authority; and capitalize on the potential of prayer. Whew! That is a mouthful! But, friends, His message to us is clear. We are in a race. We are surrounded by people who don't know Jesus. And, to add to all of this, people are watching the race. Our race! They are looking to see who we really are. They are watching to see if we will finish the race and, maybe, as they watch us as we maneuver the course and cross the finish line, they might see something that makes them wonder, "Does the Christian life really make a difference?" Although you might be a little out of breath, you will exclaim, "You better believe it!"

Though we will trek through valleys, climb steep mountains, and traverse rolling hills, we must keep on running. Despite our circumstances and the obstacles we encounter, we must look ahead and continue the race that is set before us. Yes, we might stumble and fall. We, most assuredly, will grow weary. We might even come in last. But God has called us to run. When our sunny race day turns into rain or when our side begins to cramp, we must keep our feet moving; we can't throw in the towel. We haven't finished yet! Our legs may grow tired and our breath may become labored, but our faith must never fail us. Remember Peter's stubborn perseverance, and keep in mind Job's steadfast loyalty when the race seemed impossible. Times were tough, but their faith was never lost. In order to run the race with resolve and keep our faith strong during hardships, let us keep our eyes on Jesus, the author and finisher of our faith. Just remember the example Jesus has given. And did you notice? When Jesus crossed His finish line, He sat down at the right hand of God the Father!

Right now, Jesus is watching us. He is cheering us on. And He will be waiting for you and me. As we cross the finish line, He Himself will welcome us. "Well done, good and faithful servant."

As of this moment, it is our turn. The starter has cocked the pistol. We have taken our place at the starting point. The starter's pistol has just signaled that it's time to run. We're off! I will see you at the finish line!

STUDY QUESTIONS

The First Chapter—Ready to Run: An Introduction

1. Where were you when you heard about the Twin Towers? How did you feel?

2. What did you think when you heard about the courage of Todd Beamer and the rest of the passengers on board Flight 93?

3. Why do you suppose they decided to storm the cockpit?

4. Why is it important to take action when you see a wrong being committed?

5. When you are faced with a situation that calls for action, do you stay in your seat or do you get up and move?

6. If you stay in your seat, what keeps you there?

7. If you get up and move, what do you do?

8. What do runners do to prepare for a race? How does this parallel preparing for "the race?"

9. What do we need to do to stay ready to run?

10. In life, are you standing at the starting line, ready to run? Or are you up in the crowd, watching the others run the race?

The Second Chapter—The Litmus Test

1. Has someone ever told you they believe one thing but their actions say something different?

2. How does it make you feel when a person says one thing but does another?

3. Why is it important for our actions to match our words?

4. Why do we struggle with this?

5. When you're faced with trials or hardships, how do you fare? Do you pass or fail the test?

6. Think of a time you have been sifted by Satan. What happened?

7. If you failed, what could you have done differently?

8. If you passed, how did you do so?

9. The next time you are faced with a test, what will be different?

10. What, specifically, will you do now to ensure you can pass the test next time?

The Third Chapter—To Love Like Jesus

1. Define love.

2. Recall a time when you have felt loved. What was that like?

3. Recall a time when you have made someone else feel loved. How did they respond?

4. Has there ever been a time you have purposefully refused an opportunity to love someone?

5. Why do we pass up opportunities to love one another?

6. Why is it difficult to have this mindset all the time?

7. Why did Jesus place so much emphasis on loving our neighbors?

8. How does loving our neighbors communicate God's love?

9. Name two ways you can demonstrate love to your spouse.

10. Name two ways you can demonstrate love to your children.

The Fourth Chapter—A Kingdom Plan

1. Name your blessings.

2. How can you use what you have to glorify God?

3. Why does God want us to focus on our blessings?

4. What do we deserve? Why has God chosen *not* to give us that?

5. Do you think God has a plan for your life?

6. Are you currently doing whatever it takes to figure out that plan?

7. What is God's plan for your life?

8. Why is it significant to remember, "Give us this day our daily bread"? Why did God tell the people to only gather the manna they needed that day?

9. Do you worry about tomorrow?

10. What actions can we take to focus more on today and less on tomorrow?

The Fifth Chapter—To Walk in Your Shoes

1. What is the meaning of the Shakespeare quote that begins this chapter? "He jests at scars that never felt a wound."

2. What is the difference in sympathy and empathy, in your own words?

3. What does it mean to walk in another man's shoes?

4. How can we do this?

5. Why is it important to do this?

6. What role does compassion play?

7. Why does God want us to be sensitive to others' circumstances, situations, and pain?

8. Have you ever been the recipient of compassion? How did it feel?

9. Have you ever shown compassion for someone else? How did they respond?

10. What can we do to communicate sympathy, empathy, and compassion to others?

The Sixth Chapter—To Love, Honor, and Cherish

1. Why does God value marriage?

2. What value does our society place on marriage? Why?

3. How can we, as Christians, help to restore the concept of marriage?

4. Why are matters within marriage so difficult to discuss?

5. How can we keep ourselves free from becoming entangled in extramarital affairs?

6. What does "honor" look like in a marriage? How can you honor marriage?

7. Why did God give us marriage?

8. Why do we struggle with "keeping the marriage bed pure"?

9. How can we overcome a past sexual sin?

10. What can we do to safeguard our marriages now and in the future?

The Seventh Chapter—The Unattainable Illusion

1. Define contentment.

2. Are you content? Why or why not?

3. How can we overcome the Joneses' Syndrome?

4. Name the blessings you left out in Chapter 4.

5. List what you think Osama bin Laden deserves. Now list what you think you deserve.

6. Why do we keep on chasing after the things of this world?

7. How do we feel when we attain those things we were chasing?

8. Why do we think things or achievements will bring us happiness?

9. How do we find real contentment?

10. What does that feel like?

The Eighth Chapter—Follow the Leader

1. Who are the leaders in your life? Name them.

2. Do you follow them, or do you question them?

3. Why does God give us the directive to follow those in leadership?

4. Are you a leader? If so, in what capacity do you lead?

5. How do you feel when others follow?

6. How do you feel when those under you go their own direction without regard to your instruction?

7. How does this relate to God and to the leaders in your own life?

8. How can we communicate to those we follow that we trust them?

9. What can we do to be effective leaders?

10. What can we do to be effective followers?

The Ninth Chapter—To Know the Truth

1. Define truth. Name examples of things you know to be true.

2. Define false. Names examples of things you know to be false.

3. Why is it important to know the truth?

4. Why is it essential in our Christian lives to be able to spot a false teaching?

5. How can we do this?

6. Why do we get swept up by falsehoods from time to time?

7. How can we get out from underneath its grip?

8. How can we prevent ourselves from being swept away?

9. What are steps we can take to ensure we follow what's true and run from what's false?

10. How can we be a light shining into darkness? What will happen if we do this?

The Tenth Chapter—A Relationship of Praise

1. Why were we created?

2. Define relationship.

3. Define praise, in your own words.

4. What do we need to do to have a relationship of praise with God?

5. Why is it important to have clean and pure hearts?

6. How can we maintain this level of purity?

7. What does the author mean by "the fruit of the lips"?

8. Why did Paul remind us "to do good and to share with others"?

9. How are "doing good and sharing" related to praising God?

10. How can your life be a blessing to God? In what ways can your life bless God? Name them.

The Eleventh Chapter—The Strength of Submission

1. How does the world view the term "submission"?

2. How does God see this word?

3. Why is it important to demonstrate a submissive spirit?

4. To whom should you submit? Name them.

5. Do you submit? If yes, how? If no, why not?

6. How does mutual submission affect the church? How does the lack of mutual submission affect the church?

7. How does mutual submission affect your home, specifically? How does the lack of mutual submission affect your home?

8. What does it feel like when everyone is leading?

9. What specifically can you do to be more submissive in church and in your home?

10. What can you do to show submission to God?

The Twelfth Chapter—The Potential of Prayer

1. Do you pray? How often?

2. What do you pray for most often?

3. How important is prayer to your life as a Christian? Why is it?

4. Do you truly believe in the power and the potential of prayer?

5. Do you pray for others? If so, in what regard?

6. Have you ever prayed for the conscience and conduct of others?

7. Why does God's Word tell us to do this?

8. How can you become more vulnerable to others regarding your prayer life?

9. Do you utilize the full potential of prayer? Why or why not?

10. How can we develop stronger, more faith-filled prayer lives?

The Thirteenth Chapter—The Race of Faith Finish Line: Final Thoughts

1. What area discussed in this book do you struggle with the most?

2. What can you do to improve?

3. Which do you feel is the one, most important lesson you have learned from this book?

4. How can you put this lesson into practice? What will it take to apply what you've learned?

5. Are you ready to run?